CIVIC QUARTER LIBRARY
LEEDS METROPOLITAN UNIVERSITY

Beckett Park Learning Centre
~~Leeds LS6 3QS~~

Items should be returned on or before the last date shown below
All items are subject to recall if required by another reader. The loan
period may be shortened from that given below and, in these
circumstances, you must return the item by the revised due date
indicated on the recall notice which we send you.

Charges are levied for the late return of items.

Renewal may be made by personal application, in writing or by telephoning
(0113) 283 3164 and quoting the barcode number below.

Date Due	Date Due	Date Due	Date Due
	18 SEP 2014		
09 JAN 03			
20. MAR 03			
MAY 03			

BENCHMARKING
FOR PEOPLE MANAGERS

John Bramham graduated from Manchester University in 1966 with a degree in psychology. He progressed through various gas companies in the UK, starting in industrial relations and working in recruitment and training. In the 1970s he was manpower planning manager with British Gas HQ in London before becoming industrial relations manager in Newcastle upon Tyne in the 1980s. In 1989 he was appointed director of personnel at North Eastern Gas, based in Leeds. In 1994 he joined the team of managers working to establish a new company ethos in TransCo, now part of BG International. In 1997 he became an independent consultant when he formed the HR Group. He is a fellow of the Institute of Personnel and Development, a fellow of the Manpower Society, and a graduated member of the British Psychological Society. His previous books include the best-selling *Practical Manpower Planning*, first published in 1975, and *Human Resource Planning*, the second edition of which came out in 1994 (both are published by the IPD).

developing practice

The Institute of Personnel and Development is the leading publisher of books and reports for personnel and training professionals and students and for all those concerned with the effective management and development of people at work. For full details of all our titles please telephone the Publishing Department on 0181 263 3387.

BENCHMARKING FOR PEOPLE MANAGERS

$\mathcal{P}$

John Bramham

INSTITUTE OF PERSONNEL AND DEVELOPMENT

Dedication:
To all those people who have put up with me all these years

© John Bramham, 1997

First published in 1997

Design by Paperweight
Typeset by Action Typesetting, Gloucester
Printed in Great Britain by
the Cromwell Press, Wiltshire

British Library Cataloguing in Publication Data
A catalogue record for this book is available from the British
Library

ISBN 0-85292-669-3

INSTITUTE OF PERSONNEL
AND DEVELOPMENT

IPD House, Camp Road, London SW19 4UX
Tel: 0181 971 9000   Fax: 0181 263 3333
Registered office as above. Registered Charity No. 1038333
A company limited by guarantee. Registered in England No. 2931892

CONTENTS

PREFACE

I have always believed that behind all new management fads sold with enthusiasm (and not a little hype) there are a few simple ideas struggling to get out. Taking one example, Tom Peters in 1982 was probably the first to get famously into print with the idea that organisations should stay close to their customers and stick to the business they are good at. Now we all remember the subsequent failures of his 'excellent' companies – not the strength of those basic and simple ideas. It is important that the ideas in books become internalised and affect the way people think and act when they are managing (or to use a more modern term – coaching).

It is the same with benchmarking. At root, benchmarking is simply about making comparisons with other organisations and then learning the lessons that those comparisons throw up. Obviously, the better the partners are at a given task the more you can learn from them. In rapidly changing times it is easy to rest on your previous excellent performance and become complacent. Benchmarking against good performers is one way of guarding against that.

I hope that in Chapter 1 the reader will understand the argument for benchmarking and see the links with total quality and the importance of information technology. We can only guess at the change that will come for jobs and careers from the greater use of expert systems. In Chapter 2 I offer a simple model or framework for benchmarking, with the various stages and types of benchmarking discussed. In Chapter 3 it is suggested that you must know where you are currently and suggests a number of tools to use. Culture, values and people are described in Chapter 4 and the importance of teamwork and overcoming NIH (not invented here) is discussed. Chapter 5 considers process and the idea that by combining jobs into their key natural processes a more responsive and quicker delivery can be gained than by traditional functional structures. Chapter 6 recognises that by and large HR adds value to assets rather than products or services, while in Chapter 7 we discuss metrics, the numbers of benchmarking. Chapter 8 is about choosing partners with whom to compare. Chapter 9 is about benchmarking HR and Chapter 10 is concerned with the wider strategic task of benchmarking HR activities across the whole organisation. In Chapter 11 we discuss managing a pilot and the importance of good project management, and in Chapter 12 the role of consultants. Chapter 13 looks at why things go wrong. Chapter 14 is concerned with business process re-engineering (BPR), which can have an important role in benchmarking even though it has had a bad press. Appendix 1 is reproduced with the permission of Saratoga (Europe) and is a comprehensive list of possible HR benchmarks. Appendix 2 is a list of contact addresses.

This book is intended to be easily accessible. I hope I have avoided the display of complexly presented knowledge for its own sake. We have all noticed how smoothly everything seems to go when looking in textbooks or attending conferences and seminars. Do beware those wonderful-sounding presentations of 'how we did it in xyz company'. By and large they did not! I recall speaking at a conference some years ago and had listened to expert after expert extolling the virtues of how they ran industrial relations. Everything was neat and orderly and they never lost. It did not sound like real 1970s IR to me! I began by saying that the most common events in the cauldron of IR, were not strategic thinking, careful planning and good communications. They were politics, uncertainty, fear and panic. It went down well at the time. You would have thought that having swallowed all the 'excellence' stuff telling us how good IBM, Hewlett Packard, Disney and Digital Equipment were, and then having witnessed the nemesis, we might have learnt. Apparently we have not. We still go to overpriced glib and glossy presentations and look for simple solutions in textbooks!

So when reading this book have beside you a bowl of salt that is essential on all such occasions – whether reading management books, or attending conferences or seminars. You can then have 15 pinches ready – one to be taken with each chapter. The remainder of the bowl you can keep for all the other 'how to do it' experiences that you will be put through over the years.

If you internalise 'authorisation steps', 'hand-offs', 'hand-ons', 'pass overs' and 'performance gaps' you will be getting value from this book. There is also organisational mapping, 'NIH' (not invented here), and the importance of strategy and the role of detail, not grandly expressed ideas, in defining and achieving it. To these must be added the ideas of a process-led organisation that I see as a natural extension of the gradual move of organisational power from producers to customers that is taking place in most of industry, commerce and government services. Bureaucracy is essential in large complex communities, but we have gradually let the politics of bureaucracies take over. We have been concerned with making peace and managing relations within the organisations, while forgetting the customer outside and the need to stick to our core business.

If you understand some or all of these things then I will be satisfied, but the real work as ever is up to you. I wish you the best of luck with it.

John Bramham
April 1997

ACKNOWLEDGEMENTS

My greatest debt is to all those people in the former and present gas companies who gave me the opportunity to practise the ideas covered in this text. In particular I would like to mention Harry Moulson, formerly managing director of British Gas TransCo, and two of his directors – Steve Copley and John Dilks – who were particularly helpful to me.

In writing this text I have received incalculable help from John Clayton of Senn Delaney Leadership Corporation, David Batey and his staff at Coopers & Lybrand, Jo Barnet of the British Quality Foundation, Trevor Toolin of Pilat, Andrew Ward of the Ward Dutton Partnership and Jac Fitz-Enz and Richard Phelps of the Saratoga Institute and Saratoga (Europe) respectively. I should also not forget my various friends in the IPD and the British Psychological Society, who continue to provide help in many ways. A particular mention is due to the excellent work of the Manpower Society and its offshoot 'FiSSing' in the benchmarking areas.

In addition I have read all of the texts mentioned in the references and where I have quoted from them directly I have credited them in the text. Over the years ideas and models become mingled in one's mind and it is possible that I have omitted someone. If so, I apologise and any corrections can be made in any reprint.

My wife, Susan, helped enormously with the typescript and gave the necessary encouragement to complete the task. My children, Helen and Wendy, were also bribed to help with production tasks. Peter Riley, Ian Nicholls and Iris Nicholls read the completed typescript and Martin Lea helped with the research. All made many helpful suggestions and corrections. I should like to pay tribute to them.

Finally it would be remiss of me not to recognise the contribution made by Matthew Reisz in the IPD Publishing

Department. His extensive knowledge and professionalism are beyond measure.

This book has been greatly improved as a result of all these people's kind efforts. However, for all their help, the finished product is my own responsibility. I hope that the reader finds it helpful.

1

INTRODUCTION TO BENCHMARKING

What this book aims to do

Benchmarking is simply the systematic process of comparing your business with others, or parts of your own with one another to test how you stand and to see whether change is needed. Usually you will identify examples of superior performance, and when you do you should set out to emulate and even better them.

Change is rapid and experience is widely spread, so no longer can one go to a single company and see 'how it is done'. People used to visit the great industries in England in the nineteenth century, Ford in the 1920s, or General Electric or IBM up to the 1970s to see 'how it was done', the 'it' being some activity or process that was presumed to be the best. Now the best can be found anywhere, and you have to search and measure constantly to find it. This is benchmarking.

Innovative adaptation has been around as long as industry itself. The Americans who came to England in the nineteenth century (and the Britons who made the return trip more recently!) or the Japanese who copied Western technology were in a sense benchmarking. What is different now, though, is that the successful organisation is as likely to benchmark as the one that knows it has ground to make up. The reason for the difference is that no one has a monopoly on excellence and leadership in business. It is a fragile commodity, easily lost. This is the subject of the remainder of this chapter, and Chapter 2.

This brings with it the problem of whether ideas from

outside the organisation, or even the department, will be implemented, assuming they meet a need. The 'not-invented-here' mentality leads to the waste of many good ideas because the organisation is not ready for them. So the cultural problem of knowledge transfer, of overcoming the 'not invented here' syndrome, is one of the key features of this text; it is discussed in Chapter 4, 'Culture Values and People'.

My book is directed at people managers – perhaps managers of HR/personnel departments – but could equally apply to line managers, all of whom have an HR responsibility. The book aims to put some structure around what benchmarking is and explain both why it has emerged at the present time and what is driving organisations to become involved in it. It will go through the simple comparison of ratios in Chapter 7 on metrics to more complex business areas in Chapter 9, and will finally press the case for HR to be involved in formulating strategy in organisations in Chapter 10. This is often not easy, because in many organisations HR is not well placed to take such initiatives; but there are steps that can be undertaken. One such is to demonstrate a professional knowledge and understanding of benchmarking techniques. But the techniques are not enough. The manager who can show the importance of mapping where the organisation is will be listened to, and this is discussed in Chapter 3, 'Mapping'.

It is also important to concentrate on adding value and to recognise that much of what HR does adds value only in an indirect way. This issue of 'adding value' is the subject of Chapter 6. HR people have a reputation for avoiding anything numerical, but benchmarking has an important numerical thread running through it. The HR manager can also know about the right way to choose benchmarking partners, and the strengths and weaknesses of various approaches, particularly in the judicious use of consultants and outsourcing. Finally, the HR manager can show the case for benchmarking HR activities, particularly those of business-wide concern, such as training, appraisals and reward strategy. These are the areas discussed in Chapter 10 on strategic issues, Chapter 11 on 'Piloting the Project', and Chapter 13, when we shall look at why benchmarking projects can fail. I shall discuss all of this while striving to overcome the failing inherent in much benchmarking and 'business process re-engineering' of the late 1980s and early 1990s: the failure to understand and account for people properly. All of these aspects will be covered by this text.

At the operational level it is possible to benchmark such criteria as departmental budgets, departmental productivity, absence or recruitment and training costs. At the business level, the concern will be directed towards the way people are recruited or trained. Here the concentration will be less on individual tactical issues than on how things are done that require business-wide solutions. If you are benchmarking in order to contemplate outsourcing a particular activity (such as pre-screening graduate applicants), it is necessary to ensure that any proposals have the support of other organisation members. It may also be appropriate to consider strategic concerns that will involve board-level decisions; if that is the case, benchmarking must have the support of the senior decision-makers of the organisation. These are the issues that will be explored more fully in Chapter 2.

The race for competitive advantage

The pace of change has been quickening inexorably for at least a generation. This much is well known, but what is not so clearly understood are the implications of that change. What was originally regarded as a sound business can suddenly find itself without customers or users of its services. This has led managers to contemplate how they might stay up with the leaders. What is it that will provide them with the knowledge of where the market is going and what the next product innovation might be, or what new service might be demanded of the organisation? What might alert the organisation to new pressures that will lead to apparently arbitrary changes with devastating consequences for the organisation? How can these changes be spotted? How can the organisation stay ahead? This is the environment in which the modern manager must manage.

From total quality to benchmarking

Why, then, is 'total quality' not a sufficient way forward? There is a constant requirement to improve competitiveness because the ease of modern communications means that no business can feel itself safe and isolated from the strains of the market-place. Internal measurement has long been accepted. Whether it was in sales, production, profit ratios, etc there was recognition of the need to measure performance and seek ways of improving it. So budgets were set and then shaved to try to get that bit of extra performance. This led to the incremental changes inherent in 'total quality' and trying to get those few extra decimal places of percentage achievement out of the business. Work study is an early example of that approach in practice. People were encouraged to forgo past working practices and work a little more efficiently, using new methods or technology for a little extra pay. This is incremental change and it is still the driving force behind practices such as quality management. The Japanese have built a very successful economy on continuous improvement of this nature and they even have a word for it – 'Kaizen'.

The requirement for change did not relent and the pressure built up on organisations year-on-year to respond. These were driven by the market-place in two ways. First, and most obviously, companies were required to improve quality or reduce costs (and usually both) simply to stand still and continue to have a market presence. There was a second effect for which people in the organisations were not prepared. Although the market-place as such did not exist for some of these services (most public services for example) pressure by financial constraints was put on them to change. The 'death by a thousand cuts' had begun. This was partly because employment costs swallowed up an increasingly large part of the budget and inevitably other costs had to be reduced (or at least not increased in line with perceived need and inflation). Employees of these organisations, in taking a greater share of the resources available in terms of wages and benefits, contributed to the apparent paradox where increasing financial provision (after discounting inflation) still led to real cuts in services. This is an analysis that will be familiar to those working in most organisations and it is particularly relevant in the public health, education, police and other public services. Benchmarking emerged out of this requirement to make comparisons with other departments and then with other organisations as a way of keeping abreast of the changes taking place.

In attempting to meet these cost and quality pressures, organisations placed more and more emphasis on achieving these changes while expecting employees or clients to deliver more. It was inevitable that the situation could not continue indefinitely. The relentless reduction in the numbers of basic skilled employees was accompanied by a growing managerial and supervisory group. Many organisations during the period from 1970 to 1985 saw huge growth in their 'managerial' workforce. This happened because the need to improve quality or reduce overhead costs in the traditional way was always accompanied by the appointment of an investigating and enforcement manager. But the stresses being placed on the old structure were stretching it to breaking point.

Organisations therefore needed to identify the gaps in performance to identify where things were going awry. In this situation, benchmarking offers a possible way out. It is becoming difficult, if not impossible, to achieve the 'cuts' that are required within existing structures. New ways have to be found to meet the business requirements of the future. Whether it is by amalgamating jobs, as in one oil company, or multiskilling as within the car industry, or outsourcing – as is happening within many organisations – we all have to look at processes. But first we have to understand what is meant by a 'process' and come to terms with the implications of it. This is the subject of Chapter 5, 'A Process Organisation'.

All we can be sure of is that the way in which work was organised yesterday is probably no longer appropriate. All of this has implications for how organisations view the way they manage their employees (command and control v empowerment discussed in Chapter 4) and for changing the way organisations work and view themselves, as discussed in Chapter 5. The answer to the question posed above, as to why total quality is not a sufficient solution to business problems lies in the extent to which incremental change is regarded as inherent in total quality, and the extent to which benchmarking can identify the need for step change. This recognition of the need, in some circumstances, for step change as opposed to incremental change has led to total quality gradually re-inventing itself to accommodate the strengths of benchmarking.

A shared vision

What, then, can be done in practice? Most successful organisations maintain success in three ways, by

☐ having a clear and shared vision of what the organisation is about
☐ constant attention to detail
☐ having employees who are willing to change.

It is no use having a vision that is not shared by all those responsible for delivering it. Time and again our experience gives us examples of a fine-sounding vision proclaimed as one enters an organisation, only to find that it is not matched in practice by what happens when as customers we come to use its services, or as employees we wish to deliver them.

The second of these three important aspects recognises that managers must be continually checking how the organisation is running. Whether it is the finances or debt control or delivery times or product or service quality or absence control or labour turnover – there must be a constant search to monitor the health of the organisation and look for possible improvements. All of these matters are indicators of whether business is going as the organisation intends. Anything that shows that such key matters are declining requires attention, and any general decay across a number of such items requires urgent attention, perhaps involving strategic solutions. Finally, without the support of employees who are fully committed to change – and indeed see change as their constant companion at work – no organisation can thrive for long and no change can be carried through completely. This constant measuring of success against an agreed vision, supported by employees who carry out changes as required, neatly sums up what benchmarking requires in order to achieve its aims.

What is benchmarking?

At its simplest level, benchmarking consists of comparing your organisation with another. In this way you can decide whether your organisation's performance is in some way falling short of the standard against which you compare yourself. This standard is the 'benchmark'. Benchmarking can be undertaken in a variety of situations. In an organisation-wide context all the key factors can be benchmarked. Such items as financial performance, profit and loss, cash flow, investment, sales, production and productivity are all subject to regular benchmarking within industry and commerce.

Different approaches to benchmarking

This is a book for people managers and it is on this area of benchmarking that we shall concentrate. The people manager may be a line manager with people who report to him or her, or an HR or personnel manager whose interest in benchmarking may be somewhat different. The line manager may well be interested in his own department and how it is performing. Such aspects as employee costs, sales or production targets are important areas to benchmark. The HR manager will have a similar interest as a manager of people. An HR manager will want benchmarking analysis of recruitment procedures, numbers employed, staff productivity (such as days training per trainer) and so on. Examples are shown in Table 1. These are largely matters internal to the HR department and need not involve other managers.

The HR manager may also have a responsibility to keep company HR policy at least abreast with, if not ahead of, the field. One way of meeting this responsibility is to undertake comparisons with other organisations across the field of HR policy and practice – not just within the HR function. So total employees, productivity levels, sickness and accident rates are obvious targets. These are also areas in which other managers have a keen strategic interest.

This entails the HR department becoming involved in benchmarking as a key strategic player in the organisation as a whole – not just within the HR manager's own department. Examples of such items are shown in Table 2 and will be

Table 1

TARGET AREAS FOR BENCHMARKING
THE HR DEPARTMENT

- ☐ Manpower.
- ☐ Absence levels.
- ☐ Productivity.
- ☐ Training costs.
- ☐ Days training per trainer.
- ☐ Recruitment costs per recruit.
- ☐ Time spent on recruitment process.
- ☐ Occupational health costs per employee.
- ☐ Catering and welfare costs per employee.
- ☐ Employee relations costs per employee.
- ☐ All major HR procedures, policies and guidelines.

Table 2

TARGET AREAS FOR BENCHMARKING
ORGANISATION-WIDE ISSUES – NUMERICAL

- ☐ Total employees.
- ☐ Productivity levels.
- ☐ Sickness, accidents and absence.
- ☐ Sales per employee.
- ☐ Profit and loss.
- ☐ Cash flow.
- ☐ Investment.

discussed more in Chapter 7 on Metrics and Chapter 9 dealing with HR and a strategic role. These areas are particularly suitable for numerical analysis. The numerics of benchmarking are called 'metrics' in benchmarking jargon and are discussed in Chapter 7.

Less obvious are those areas where benchmarking is valuable but where the returns are inevitably more difficult to achieve. This involves key strategic areas of culture and staff attitudes to the organisation, its value systems and approaches to management, methods of appraisal and development and the uses made of such schemes. Reward mechanisms can also tell us a great deal about how the organisation functions. Such a study will reveal any conflicts that may exist between policy and practice. These matters are developed more fully in Chapter 10, but at this stage they provide examples of the possible conflicts that may be identified.

It is not uncommon for organisations to have policies proclaiming that individual achievement will be recognised, that entrepreneurship is valued, and that excellence will be rewarded, and all employees will be treated fairly. In practice it is not unusual to find long grades with automatic progression, along with trade union negotiated increases for everyone. There is not necessarily anything wrong with such an approach, but it is contrary to the stated policy. Excellence cannot be encouraged if the reward mechanisms (including non-monetary rewards) value mediocrity. It is possible to highlight such internal policy conflicts through benchmarking and decide a way forward that suits your organisation, and that works towards policy and practice being in strategic harmony.

Benchmarking beyond simple comparison

The foregoing comments highlight one of the early decisions that will have to be taken concerning benchmarking. It is entirely possible to undertake comparisons of key numerical data with other organisations. Areas of concern can be identified and sorted out. For example, it may be found that absence is high in a particular location, or that productivity is low; these problems can be considered within the unit and resolved.

This first level of benchmarking is entirely respectable and, contrary to what other texts may say, there is no reason to go further for its own sake. The organisation may already have been through a series of significant changes and you may decide that now is not the moment for more. If, however, you

Table 3

TARGET AREAS FOR BENCHMARKING
ORGANISATION-WIDE ISSUES – STRATEGIC

☐ Culture.
☐ Value systems.
☐ Development and appraisal.
☐ Approaches to reward.
☐ Management training.
☐ Recruitment as part of a process.

decide that significant change is needed, that change may involve benchmarking the whole organisation rather than just a department. If that is the case you will inevitably be drawn into those areas listed in Tables 1, 2 and 3. To analyse the organisation in this way you need to be able to identify those matters that are crucial to the organisation, such as those listed in Table 3. Some activities affect the bottom line and some do not. This means knowing what makes the organisation 'tick'; what drives performance and, beyond that, profit or service. It is important that this exercise is undertaken and its results shared as widely as possible. If you look at the list in Table 3 you will see that it is quite different from that in Table 2. The contrast between sickness levels and value systems could hardly be greater. They are, however, inextricably linked, as will be discussed in Chapter 3 on mapping, and Chapter 10 on strategy.

This area is related to the general cultural issues that inevitably emerge. The more significant the change that is required the more important it is to consider culture, attitudes and approaches to management. It is also possible to benchmark in these areas. By a combination of asking questions of benchmarking companies, employee surveys, 360-degree approaches, and so on, benchmarks can be established for the sort of organisation you wish yours to become. Of course, there is a danger here. Comparisons of this nature are drawn up from answers to questions and are therefore heavily judgmental.

There are differences of opinion about the use to which such results should be put. Judgements vary from department to department and from person to person. One organisation (Electoral Reform Ballot Services 1997) discourages clients from using data for benchmarking across different cultures because of the problem of false comparisons. However, the Business Excellence Model (British Quality Foundation 1996) is predicated on an assumption that comparisons of this nature are valid. Indeed the European award system, which is part of this model, depends upon it.

The decision you take will depend on what your organisation's needs are. Whatever approach is decided upon in your own context you need to understand that some data and some comparisons are more robust than others. If that is done you will not come badly unstuck. This area of culture, values, visions and approaches to managing people is covered more completely in Chapter 4.

Benchmarking activities

It quickly becomes apparent that if significant change is required it cannot be achieved without an analysis of the work being done. For example, many organisations have faced the paradox of pressure on budgets and a need to reduce costs (and therefore often people) while at the same time looking at increased demand for output which would typically be expected to mean a requirement for more people. This vice-like grip is familiar to everyone in business, commerce and services these days. To some extent the issues can be looked at tactically.

Having established the required benchmarks it is possible to 'tinker' with the organisation and for the necessary changes to be made. If the pressure continues however (and it will!) sooner or later it becomes necessary to look at the work being done to see whether it can be dispensed with or reduced in some way. So in recruitment, for example, it may be unnecessary to write individual acknowledgement letters to all candidates when an acknowledgement card filled in by the candidate would suffice. Perhaps some training could be undertaken by line managers following a prescribed format. It is also important to understand what adds value – what the customer pays for. The customer may be willing to pay for a high quality service that comes from professionally trained workers, and this may be a key selling point. Unfortunately, the customer is unlikely to be impressed that you have spent money on a development and appraisal scheme, or on your recruitment programme – those aspects will rightly be regarded as your own problems. These are all ways that process and values can be analysed, and they are discussed more fully in Chapters 4, 5 and 6.

Benchmarking partners

The more that the organisation becomes involved in benchmarking the more limited are internal comparisons likely to become. This is not to say that comparisons with other divisions or departments within the organisation have no value. They may be all that are available, and they can lead to significant change. It is always a good idea to exhaust internal possibilities first. If you are part of a large industry, or part of a conglomerate grouping, internal partners are easier to find – and perhaps more ready to provide comparison analyses in a format that you can both use.

The danger is one of complacency. Viewed from a relatively narrow standpoint, the organisation may appear to be in good order. However, if viewed from another perspective it may be that productivity levels, costs, cash flow, absence, and so on are all in need of attention. It is to be hoped that if this is the case other signals will be available to warn you. For example, declining market share, rising recruitment costs, increasing absence rates, delivery failures and the rest are, particularly when taken together, signs that something may be amiss. Choosing partners is a difficult area and there are no right or wrong methods. However, solid advice is available in Chapter 8, which discusses the matter in more detail.

The need for support

At all levels of benchmarking you will probably require some degree of managerial support as well as resource allocation. If you are a director of HR you can achieve significant changes within the HR department. The use of colleagues and friendly companies will allow benchmarking of many of the HR drivers. Such aspects as employee costs, absence levels, training, development schemes, and so on could all be improved by fairly rudimentary comparisons.

However, if you are not a director you may need your directors' support; if you are a director you will have responsibilities that go beyond your own department. In either of these circumstances you need to be able to build support, and this issue is discussed in Chapter 11 on project pilots. Related to this aspect is the appropriate use of consultants. At routine levels they are not necessary, although they can always be useful. The difficulty will be to keep control of their efforts so that they meet your needs – and your ability to pay their costs. These issues are explained more fully in Chapter 12.

Business process re-engineering

This book is not about business process re-engineering (BPR). BPR can be seen as a natural offshoot of benchmarking that has received much criticism. The objectives of BPR are 'to be the best' and to adopt 'world class process-led organisations'. This search for 'best in class' is fair enough and the constant reference to 'process' is something that this book also stresses (see Chapter 5). The problem seems to be that BPR has become strongly associated with harsh downsizing and making dramatic and significant change while seeming to neglect the strategic and people implications of implementing change. This sort of BPR could be the result of wrongly applied re-engineering efforts. The failure to account properly for strategic impact and to take people along with the change may again be the fault of misapplication of techniques by over- zealous managers. Whatever the cause, changes have taken place in organisations that have been misconceived and they have become closely associated with BPR. These areas are discussed in Chapter 14.

The problems of benchmarking

What problems are you likely to encounter? Clearly, lack of support can be one issue, and shortage of resources another.

The identification of reliable partners is a problem that can waste time and money. Proper choice of project managers and project teams is very important, as is benchmarking the best area to establish the provenance of the process; this is considered in Chapter 11. You may choose a bad consultant and become side-tracked, as discussed in Chapter 12. You may fail to link strategies effectively so that strains and breakdowns result from the inevitable conflict, as referred to in Chapters 9 and 10.

The advice of this book, however, is that the major issues to be overcome are in the culture and human relations fields. If the organisation has barriers that prevent it from appreciating and accepting the relevance of other people's experiences and the data flowing from them, then there is little hope for benchmarking. This is the subject of Chapter 13 with its emphasis on avoiding 'proxiphobia' and the 'not invented here' (NIH) syndrome.

Information technology, customers and change

Where has all this activity come from? The first point to recognise is the importance of information technology. Computers facilitate the manipulation of large amounts of data and they have been very important in the development of benchmarking. The second point is the rise in the power of the customer. Previous generations of managers emphasised the differences that could be made to a product by enhanced production methods. But now the focus has moved outside the organisation to the customer and what the customer will pay for. Whether you are in car manufacturing or education, a significant shift is taking place towards the customer. Finally, a driving force that leads directly to benchmarking is the pace of change. Quite simply, organisations cannot expect to look to incremental change to keep themselves up to date. To survive nowadays rapid and sudden step changes are often necessary. Many organisations have been through progressive exercises to reduce budgets and cut people and now cry that 'enough is enough – we can do no more!' When that situation is reached, and yet more is needed, it is time for benchmarking – time to compare yourself with the best, either at home or abroad. Then you have to look to see how those other organisations achieve such apparent excellence – if indeed they do. The result of benchmarking brings you inevitably to ask how you propose to bring about the required changes in your own operations.

This, then, is benchmarking. Like all new approaches to management, its adherents can be accused of over-excitability when making claims for the process. There have been successes, but it is difficult to say to what extent such successes have been the result of the approaches used. Perhaps those organisations, with their assured leaders, would have made those changes with a variety of approaches.

The importance of people in benchmarking

This book, unlike many others, is written for those who believe that people make the difference between success and failure in business. People are an asset, but not as some would add, 'like any other'. People are not like money or machinery or systems. They are literally an asset with a mind of its own. Forget that at your peril! This manager may get away with ignoring the people whom the organisation employs, or that manager may meet his targets regardless of the actions taken; eventually, however, the fund of goodwill (or, admittedly, inertia) will no longer exist and then the reaction comes with a vengeance. People are not an asset 'like any other' as is often said. There are too many commentators who use such language when speaking of people. The recent trend for intrusive 'HR-speak' ('downsizing' and 'release packages', to note two current ones) is worrying and sounds dangerously like treating people as a commodity.

Summary and conclusion

Meanwhile, we are dealing with the situation we are in and it is important that organisations respond accordingly. What is going on is a considerable shaking up of business and organisations, getting them to see beyond this year's good results and to remember all the huge companies that foundered through complacency; companies that thought they were world class but soon posted huge losses as large as the gross domestic product of some countries! Commentators and writers can surely be forgiven a touch of hyperbole in suggesting ways forward. We are surely not so cynical that we cannot lift our minds to some of the possibilities that the best of us might be able to achieve under good circumstances. It is surely necessary to equip the manager with those principles for good practice. Then it is necessary to set the manager on his journey with as many signposts marked, and warning signs identified, as possible. There is, however, a reluctance in this book to have too many pretensions because the certainty is that the manager will meet a totally new situation. You must have the basic principles and then trust to your own judgement. It is also recognised that managers, particularly HR managers, are struggling for resources in the real and largely unforgiving world. Managers do things that they know are not ideal, but they do them because they can see no other way or because they do not have the power to push through alternatives. We all want to keep our jobs!

This pragmatic approach is what is suggested in this book. Benchmarking is an approach to solving the manager's problems. It seeks to show by comparison with others whether performance has fallen behind and needs to catch up. The race for competitive advantage allied with technological change is what makes benchmarking essential. But those comparisons have to be implemented to do any good, and that will require the willing support of employees. This is why a shared understanding of the organisation and its problems is important – people must be part of the exercise, not an afterthought to be manipulated. Comparing with partners is not the only way to excellent customer service, product quality and satisfied employees – but it has been shown to be a good way for many ordinary organisations that want to be better and keep up with, and perhaps ahead of, the competition.

2

APPROACHES TO BENCHMARKING

A benchmarking framework

From its first recorded use as a surveyor's term in 1842 'benchmarking' came to be the 'establishment, by rigorous and systematic measurement, of a point of reference against which performance could be measured' (OED 1994). The Economist of 18 May 1964 said that 'foreign firms fail to get orders unless they have a price advantage of at least 50%. This is the benchmark'.

From these beginnings, over the last 30 years a body of knowledge and techniques have been developed to give us benchmarking as we know it today. What, then, are the practical steps that the average people manager might reasonably be able to take? First it is necessary to understand the theory of benchmarking. An example of a procedure is shown in Figure 1. A degree of caution must be exercised with such charts. Events never fit into such neat compartments, but in practice it will help the reader to organise work and understand what has to be done. Let us go through the stages in order.

Investigating

This is the initial stage of benchmarking when a decision is made to compare various indicators, usually the important ones, with other organisations. First, it is important to set out the objectives of the exercise. Is an attempt to be made to have a cursory look at other organisations or is an in-depth study envisaged? What resources and support do you have? There is

Figure I
BENCHMARKING CYCLE

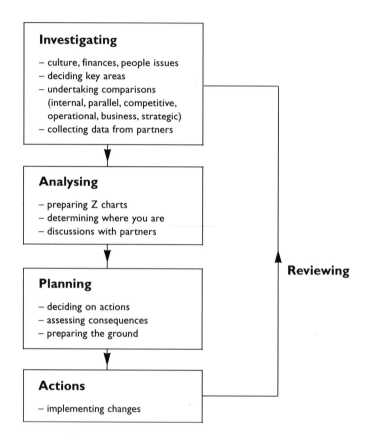

no point collecting enormous amounts of data if you do not
have the necessary support or resources to make use of them.
Remember that when the objectives of the exercise have been
decided it is possible to revisit those objectives later. The exercise may start small (which is usually the right thing to do) and
if big issues emerge it is then possible to seek support for a
wider, more in-depth exercise. Having decided the objectives of
the exercise, you need to decide what type of benchmarking is
to take place. Clearly there are various possibilities and these
will flow naturally from the objectives of the exercise. It is

Table 4
INVESTIGATING BENCHMARKING:
POSSIBLE TYPES OF BENCHMARKING

☐ Internal – comparison within the organisation.

☐ Competitive – comparison with competitors.

☐ Parallel – comparison with organisations doing same or similar tasks.

☐ Generic – comparison of key indicators with any organisation.

important to note that these approaches are not mutually exclusive and that it is possible to use different approaches for different problems. The various approaches to benchmarking can be classified as shown in Table 4, and these are discussed in more detail below.

Internal benchmarking

Internal benchmarking is where the working practices or services provided by the organisation are compared with other practices within the organisation. An explicit benchmarking target is set, and remains within the organisation. The benchmark can relate to external factors (such as customer satisfaction) but the target is intrinsic to the organisation. It is usual to compare the same or similar activities being undertaken by departments within the organisation, or by closely related organisations in the same group. Because internally driven benchmarks are being set and compared, data collection is usually less of a problem.

Competitive benchmarking

This is where direct comparisons are made with external competitors. In this case detailed specific key indicators and processes are much more difficult to benchmark because of the reluctance of an organisation to give information. For example Xerox (one of the leaders of benchmarking) would understandably be reluctant to share information on some of its key processes with Canon or Kodak!

Parallel process benchmarking

This practice refers to the benchmarking of indicators within different organisations. For example, two organisations may feel a need to compare 360-degree feedback, or even costs of training for excavating trenches, backfilling and resurfacing processes. Obviously, different organisations such as gas, water and cable communications companies are engaged in similar activities. Although the purpose may differ (one company may be laying a fibre-optic cable and another a water pipe), many of the training processes involved will be identical.

Generic benchmarking

This refers to those activities that are common to all or most organisations – such as recruitment, training, invoicing, absence rates, productivity, profit, cash flow and the like. There is scope here for significant benefits, partly because the information will be easier to collect and the likely shortfalls in performance will become readily apparent. Instead of the incremental change that may come with internal or competitor benchmarking, generic benchmarking holds the prospect of real strategic influence over key issues. This will be important if you have a practical problem in gathering support. A generic indicator may well point up the possibility of serious problems and provide the impetus needed to gain the support of senior management.

Analysing the impact within the organisation

Having looked at the type of benchmarking appropriate to the organisation, it is essential to have a view about the likely organisational impact of the change programme that may result. This can be looked at in three target areas, as shown in Table 5. Operational or first-level (also known as performance indicator) benchmarking is where the emphasis is on how a service is delivered, or on the cost of it. It could involve change to a department or even just an activity within a section. It may require the reallocation of people to other units, or simply involve sorting out training needs. This type of benchmarking is frequently regarded with disdain because of its often modest and incremental approach to change but it can have a high success rate. Because the impact is less wide ranging, beneficial change can be achieved without the need for the highest level and comprehensive support that other approaches to benchmarking may require.

Table 5
ANALYSING BENCHMARKING RESULTS:
IMPACT AREAS

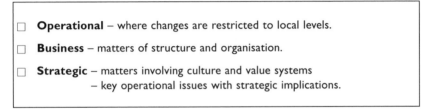

☐ **Operational** – where changes are restricted to local levels.

☐ **Business** – matters of structure and organisation.

☐ **Strategic** – matters involving culture and value systems
      – key operational issues with strategic implications.

Business or second-level (also called business performance) benchmarking relates to the impact on how the organisation is structured and how its functions and activities are managed. This is a very different area and involves and assumes top management and other functional support. It may, of course, be absolutely necessary if the type of changes that are likely to be needed arise because of structural weaknesses in the organisation.

Strategic, or third-level benchmarking deals with issues such as value systems, ethos, and matters described as 'culture'. In addition it can include key operational matters, the solution to which can be resolved only by a strategic-level approach. This can include profit, competitiveness and market share, numbers employed, large-scale redeployment or even absence control. Of course, any benefits that emerge are likely to be longer-term, and that may not be soon enough.

It is important to recognise the practical limitations as well as the advantages of each of these three approaches. Strategic-level analysis is particularly important to test out whether the organisation is in good shape. Another useful factor is that the type of information used is likely to be readily available, or can at least be derived from published data. Because it is dealing with profits, numbers of people employed and their wages, building costs and research, and so on, much of the information will be readily available in annual reports or investment analyses. It is not so easy to benchmark some aspects of HR issues because the information is not generally in the public domain. An example of the sort of information that can be benchmarked is shown in Table 6 which is divided into business areas and HR areas.

Table 6
STRATEGIC-LEVEL BENCHMARKING:
IMPACT AREAS LONG-TERM AND ORGANISATION-WIDE

☐ **General organisation issues:**

 – profit/loss

 – market share

 – productivity

 – competitiveness

 – manpower costs.

☐ **HR Issues:**

 – reward strategy

 – employee development strategy

 – empowerment v command and control.

The problem with information at the strategic level is that it has limited relevance to the jobs of the people who do the work in the organisation. It is also less accessible to many HR departments. A good organisation will have educated and informed its employees about its business needs. There is still the problem that although the information and its significance is understood, it cannot be related directly to what has to be done in 'my job' to improve the situation. There is also the difficulty that many of the issues may have their root in the strategic direction the organisation takes, in training or value systems, for example. On the plus side, change at this level –

if implemented properly – can lead to substantial benefits. The practical problems of making the connections and deciding the strategic actions are discussed more fully in Chapter 4 on 'Culture, Values and People'.

In respect of business-level issues, the advantage is that changes in organisation and structure may well be the only way that budget and resource pressures can be met. It can, however, be a disadvantage unless wide support for benchmarking has been achieved. The HR manager may conclude that improvements to efficiency can be made if changes in work distribution can be made, for example by reallocating training to professionally trained line staff. This will be difficult to achieve satisfactorily if the line departments do not agree with the HR manager's agenda. Examples of business-level issues are shown in Table 7. The important point is that 'impact' is concerned with who carries out an activity or how it is done within the business. It will look at matters that include the responsibility of functions, the relationship between departments and the devolution of operational activity from functions to process managers.

Table 7

BUSINESS-LEVEL BENCHMARKING:

IMPACT AREAS ORGANISATION-WIDE

☐ Organisation structure and relationships.

☐ Impact of changes on functions/line departments.

☐ Allocation of activities across departments.

☐ Business-wide approaches to activities.

☐ Devolution of HR activity to line.

At the operational level, the results of benchmarking can still cover a wide range of activities. Because they are dealing with the day-to-day responsibilities of a manager it is much more likely that problems can be resolved 'in house'. Examples are given in Table 8. This is true when reallocating resources within the HR department, looking at recruitment processes,

Table 8

OPERATIONAL-LEVEL BENCHMARKING:
IMPACT LIMITED WITHIN A DEPARTMENT

☐ Meeting budget needs.
☐ Reallocation of people resources.
☐ Reducing absence levels.
☐ Reducing training costs.
☐ Simplifying recruitment process and reducing costs.
☐ Evaluating jobs and checking pay levels.
☐ Simplifying and updating handbooks.
☐ Issuing self-help guidance notes to managers on HR.
☐ Activities (eg pay, unions, discipline, grievance, etc).

training delivery, absence or appraisal schemes and so on. It is much more likely that, at an operational level, problems identified through benchmarking can be considered by the manager and immediate staff with less involvement of other managers, other than to brief them on the impending changes and allowing them to comment on the proposals. Of course, the drawback of this is that operational solutions will not have the strategic impact that in truth may be required. For example, approaching high absence levels as an operational problem (such as by tinkering with procedures) may be insufficient if the high absence levels are organisation-wide and are symptomatic of motivational problems stemming from a dysfunctional culture. Another example given in Table 8 is the benchmarking of pay levels. In one sense this has been carried out by every industrial relations negotiator who has attempted to establish 'the going rate' for annual pay negotiations. These are now much more sophisticated and Incomes Data Services (IDS) publish a pay and conditions benchmark database. One word of caution is that pay is not so easily benchmarked as other items. What pay 'benchmark' will you aim for? Some organisations target the top 25 per cent (the upper quartile). Does this make sense? If you try to move to a higher benchmark your competitors have to move with you in order to keep and recruit people – so you stay in the same place! The approach to benchmarking pay has an added inflationary dimension which needs to be understood before setting benchmarks. The important point is to recognise when an operational issue has wider implications than merely for the department or unit being investigated.

Analysing results – preparing A 'Z chart'

Having considered the investigation stage you should now have a good idea of what you expect benchmarking to deliver. You have prepared your questionnaires and gathered information from your partners. You now have to analyse it. One essential task to emerge from the analysis stage is the preparation of a 'Z chart'. Benchmarking is intended to help identify a gap between the organisation's performance and that of other organisations, and then to set about closing that gap. Figure 2 represents a simplified Z chart. It is easiest to use when metrics (numbers) have been benchmarked. For example, the measure of performance in Figure 2 could be a ratio of HR staff

Figure 2

IDENTIFYING GAPS – Z CHART

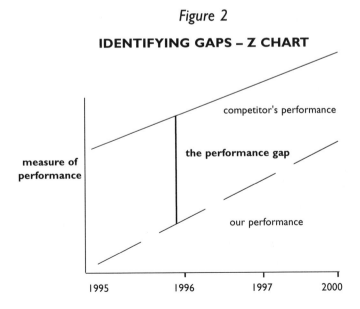

to organisation employees, or perhaps, the cost of recruitment or numbers of days training per employee. It is clearly more difficult to use other than as a conceptual framework where matters of judgement indicate a gap that is difficult to express in a numerical form. This would include, for example, cultural differences and the relative strengths of various cultures. It is important that sufficient time is spent on the analysis. It is essential that the messages contained within the data are fully understood; it is often tempting to leap to the first obvious conclusion. Without proper preparation, problems will result and opportunities will be lost to make changes that, while taking longer to have an impact, are better for the organisation in the long run. On the other hand, if the analysis phase is allowed to drag on, interest in the project can fade. You must tread a path between rushing to so-called solutions, and alternatively allowing 'paralysis by analysis' to set in.

Planning and actions

When the analysis has been completed, it is at the planning stage that decisions are taken about what, if any, actions are to be taken. It is, of course, extremely important that planning and implementation are related to the original objectives, or it must be made clear where the objectives have changed. It is also useful to recognise that a great deal of improvement and change can be implemented without massive organisational restructuring. It is entirely possible to change recruitment procedures without involving or disturbing the whole organisation. Similarly, management appraisal systems can be simplified and streamlined and this will usually be done with the welcome support of line managers. This is true of, for example, absence procedures, job evaluation, trade union handbooks, training course attendance, work study or catering services. There are always improvements that can be made in these HR areas. This is where total quality and benchmarking have something in common – the belief that changes can be achieved through incremental improvements. Much of the possibility for improvement stems from a decay in procedures whereby, over time, circumstances change and the process is no longer required, or is required, but in a different form.

Benchmarking is a way of keeping up with the need for developments of this nature.

When determining action plans it is not necessary to assume that wide-ranging, fundamental change is either necessary or appropriate. It might be – but do not overlook the obvious small-scale improvements that present themselves. It is important that you ensure that careful and thorough planning takes place before any action is taken to implement a change. The possible effects have to be considered. The analysis may have identified a problem with excess labour turnover. This may be considered through changes to working conditions or rates of pay or improved training. Each of these aspects must have action plans discussed with the users and the deliverers of the service. It may be necessary to discuss changes with trade unions if agreements are involved. It is essential that actions are fully thought through at the planning stage. This will facilitate successful implementation and lead to fewer problems at later stages.

Reviewing

When the benchmarking targets have been met, that is not the end of the matter. The need for improvement is relentless, and it is essential that benchmarking continues to test whether further developments are necessary and are taking place. One example may be given. Many organisations are investing heavily in 360-degree appraisal and development type schemes (also called multi-way feedback, and 4-way appraisal, among other names). A benchmarking process in one consultancy led to the latest thinking being implemented in their presentation and documentation. Their product was as good as any other in the market. However, one problem of 360-degree processes is the cost involved in paperwork and procedures. This cost of bureaucracy can put off many organisations from attempting 360-degree appraisal. However, what if a consultancy devised a computer-driven 360-degree appraisal system, with individuals accessing files, without the need for paper? This could be supported by computer-generated individual reports, with graphs and charts and commentary. This type of technological change is typical of something that can occur overnight and which can make a carefully worked out process look bureaucratic and outdated, and could result in a total collapse of that part of the business.

The objective therefore is not to set a standard and meet it, but to move towards best practice. This is where 'best' is itself subject to continual development as a result of changes in the market, customer's requirements and financial constraints. It is obvious at this point that we are dealing with much more than the 'simple' collection of statistics. It is true that such analysis of information can lead to setting a benchmark, but leaving the matter there cannot be sufficient. To establish a benchmark (or benchmarks) and leave it at that would be reminiscent of much of what passed for corporate planning in the 1970s. Detailed plans constructed by specialists were allowed to gather dust. For this reason, benchmarking the organisation's activities or processes must be inextricably linked with changing them to meet, and perhaps exceed, the benchmark as part of a process of continuous review.

Benchmarking in practice

Having discussed the theory, what does benchmarking look like in practice? What actually happens? We have already said that benchmarking is about comparing some feature of your department or organisation with the same or similar features in another. What this means, therefore, is taking any aspect, such as those already listed (absence, productivity, training, manpower) and comparing some parts of it with another department. Companies have approached the problem in various ways. In 1989 the HR department of a Leeds based engineering company found itself unpopular, with a reputation for costly and bureaucratic service heavily directed towards meeting union representative expectations. A survey of managers' and employees' attitudes made clear the extent of the problem. Benchmarking exercises were carried out which showed that across the industry the company was a poor performer. Benchmarking targets were established that were directed at:

- reducing costs
- improving service
- developing staff.

Using as a basis 'project tooth-tail' borrowed from the Royal Navy, resources were shifted within the HR from backroom support (that is the 'tail' of HR) to providing front line services (that is the 'teeth') for managers and their staff. For example, the number of training days per trainer increased dramatically. Service standards were improved across the board to meet benchmarked targets of performance through 'service-level agreements' that were negotiated and agreed with line managers. There was some difficulty in persuading trade unions to meet this new agenda but in time most recognised the necessity of doing so – even though the number of meetings and the time spent on them reduced enormously! Finally, development opportunities gave HR people the chance to work in line departments, and line managers to work in HR. The ultimate success of the project was seen when both groups achieved permanent jobs. By 1994 the company had moved from 11th ranking to 2nd in terms of costs and manpower levels within its group of comparator companies. Internally-measured service also improved dramatically.

Benchmarking activity began much earlier at Xerox, in fact it is possible to think of the technique as it is now practised as beginning at Xerox. The need for benchmarking was identified in the 1970s and it has now become one of three processes, along with quality and problem-solving, that are central to Xerox's 'leadership through quality programme'. The lessons learnt while introducing benchmarking are many and varied. For example, 80 per cent of benchmarking time is spent outside Xerox's industry (Camp 1993).

A different example was a north-west Borough Council HR department which undertook benchmarking in an effort to sharpen up its costs and services prior to contracts being put out to tender in 1996. This benchmarking exercise was probably one of the first to be established by a local authority. One important requirement was to find out what type of service was wanted by the department's potential future clients.

Another approach to benchmarking is found in the work of a manufacturing site team's attempt to benchmark the HR function. Not only was the company in Hull looking for the characteristics of 'best in class' operations but it was also trying to plot the evolution of the function as a whole. In 1991 a six-strong team of managers conducted an in-depth benchmarking study aimed at identifying 'best in class' chemicals manufacturing management and organisational practices world-wide. This developed into using the benchmarking approach for the HR function. Benchmarking is now seen as a tool to facilitate continuous improvement, with the most lasting impression on the HR benchmarking teams being to simplify systems – making them transparent, easy to administer and relevant to business needs.

It is also possible to use benchmarking to review practices thoroughly. An international bank, while looking at two IT departments – developments and services, took seriously the often quoted belief that the reason for the failure of benchmarking projects was a lack of consideration of the HR process. They had changed their work significantly into six end-to-end processes which were carried out by multiskilled teams, resulting in fewer hand-overs and requiring the rotation of staff between specialisms. In the transition to a new service culture, HR processes have been redesigned. They now recognise the importance of investing as much in the HR aspects of change as in the technical aspects of designing it.

An example of internal benchmarking is given by a building society. Using a toolkit of examples of good practice from around its branches its managers were encouraged to look at what they did, and to improve on it. This approach helped to make sure that the best innovations were available for use by all the other units to improve their performance. The usual approach to gathering data was used, generating information from interviews with managers and front-line staff over an initial six-month period. To ensure that the information met the society's needs and policies it was then validated by a central panel. This action resulted in a range of internally derived best practices for key processes in the business. This was on the basis that there was never one 'right' solution covering all circumstances. This bank of information is available to all branches. This approach to spreading data on benchmarking best practices was supported by 'best practice' consultants who facilitate the integration of quality work into everyday working practices (Tutcher 1994).

Competitive benchmarking is being tried by a former building society (now a bank) which with other organisations has set up relationships with competitors in a variety of consortia. The bank has developed its own five-stage model for benchmarking (1 planning, 2 networking and facilitation, 3 definition and design, 4 analysis, 5 action) (Leeman 1996).

In a separate approach, an electric company has established its HR department as a profit centre as part of a company belief in the usefulness of profit centres, particularly for support departments. The HR department has therefore been set up as a business. There remained the problem of deciding strategic guidelines to follow and it was decided that a 'central standards forum' should undertake this task. This is the approach favoured in Chapters 9 and 10 of this book. This means that delivery of services is separated from setting strategy, policy and standards. This is supported by service agreements made with managers who are free (or not) to use the service offered (Van de Vliet 1995 and IDS Study 618 January 1997).

As shown above, there are various ways in which the information can be collected. All of the reports from which the above information is drawn are in the public domain. You can, if you are interested, look up the articles so you can identify the companies and talk to their staff. You can start most effectively by obtaining the articles from public suppliers, such as the IPD. The next approach is to speak to the people involved and get them to complete a questionnaire either through the post or by visiting them. Information of the type shown in Table 9 is an example of how you can proceed. This is the way in which a picture of performance in other organisations can be built up. You will need to concentrate on those aspects of HR performance that are key to your organisation's performance, or where you know there are problems. After the initial data-gathering you will need to focus on individual activities with more pertinent analyses of the types listed in Table 10. When you have undertaken such an exercise you will begin to get a good idea of the relative strengths and weaknesses of your

Table 9

BENCHMARKING IN PRACTICE: GATHERING DETAILED INFORMATION

☐ **Data to collect includes:**

ratio of HR staff to company employees

− on training and development

− recruitment and resourcing

− industrial relations

− productivity analysis/work study

− employee services

− occupational health

− other units not listed

− total staff.

☐ **Costs**

− total personnel/HR costs

− HR employee costs

− training cost/employee

− cost of each recruit

− cost per trainee

− cost/meal delivered

− cost of IR, meeting/staff support, etc

− cost of job evaluation

− cost of occupational health.

own HR policies and also have some ideas on how you might change them. Of course, the listing will differ depending on the priorities of the organisation, but it serves to illustrate the potential of benchmarking.

Such information can be completed as a questionnaire by a

Table 10

BENCHMARKING IN PRACTICE:
GATHERING GENERAL INFORMATION

What are our key activities?

☐   Order the list of activities below recording to the extent to which they add value – to the customer

       – to the business.

☐   Of the following activities, which are you:

       – best at (maximum score = 5)

       – worst at (minimum score = 1)

       – in between, in respect to other organisations (score 2–4)?

	Add value	Worst or best
Training		
Appraisal and development		
Recruitment procedures		
Selecting key candidates		
Handling discipline and grievance		
Career planning		
Absence control		
Communicating with employees		
Work study and productivity measures		
Industrial relations		
Job evaluation		
Reward strategy		
Employee benefit programmes		

Of those marked 4 or 5, can you give more information?

respondent. An alternative approach is for a member of staff to go to the respondent and conduct an interview, asking the same questions. Another approach is to use the questionnaire as a discussion document and arrange a workshop for the purpose of benchmarking HR activity, and invite interested companies along. One problem is to ensure the comparability of data and for this reason a control figure of total costs should always be included. This is because organisations count departments differently and some items (say, costs of training) may at first seem high but on analysis it becomes apparent that different costs or numbers have been included. A control figure allows you to decide whether overall costs appear to be a problem, rather than a feature of the different way in which a company allocates its data. The detailed information of the type shown in Table 10 can also be used to gather data by questionnaire from outside organisations. One possible shortcut, at least during the early stages, is the use of consultants to provide access to data that have been collected already.

Having undertaken the analysis it is then necessary to decide what action needs to be taken towards implementation, as shown in Figure 1 under 'actions'. Sometimes the changes may be modest and can be handled in-house, and the internal toolkit approach will identify many such changes. Sometimes major rescheduling of resources may be necessary, as in the case of the Bank already mentioned. You may, for example, find an opportunity for significant cost reduction in resourcing and learning opportunities that requires the support of line managers – such as occurs through transferring operational responsibilities to the line. Clearly this is where you need to plan more carefully and ensure that benchmarking has the full support of the managers or the changes will not be made. All of which brings us to the question of who will be the catalyst for such change process? Who can, or wishes to, assume the responsibility?

Benchmarking and HR

Benchmarking is an important tool in the search for success in modern organisations. Taken together with a possible need to change how the organisation works, how its people are managed and how processes overcome barriers caused by functionality, it is possible to see the extent of the changes that need to be undertaken. The benchmarking exercise needs a champion who must ensure that it is fed and watered daily. This is a business improvement role that is available to an HR group that has its thinking right. All too often the personnel/ HR function operates in the comfort zones of establishment control, low level recruitment, training and running the company canteen. It has been pointed out that little time of the typical HR function is spent on strategic change issues of the type at the centre of benchmarking.

There is another reason why HR has a benchmarking role, and one that goes beyond the HR department itself. Many organisations have discovered that implementation does not deliver the benefits expected because of a failure properly to account for the human dimension. Personnel/human resource specialists have more opportunity than any other department to test out and consult with employees on proposed changes. It is first necessary to ensure that the organisation does not treat employees as 'just another resource' that is expected to be infinitely elastic and malleable. To do this HR must become the 'internal consultant' of the future. They have experience as catalysts across the whole organisation and someone has to provide the necessary support for projects such as benchmarking. If HR professionals are willing to give up functional control of yesterday's empire there lies ahead the prospect of increased influence and status as they become the drivers of future change.

Summary and conclusion

This chapter has moved on from a general discussion of benchmarking, setting out a framework that will help the reader recognise how simple benchmarking is as a concept, whether it is at the operational or first level, business or second level, or as a third level directed at changing and formulating organisational strategy. Internal, competitive, parallel and generic benchmarking have also been discussed – any one of which can be appropriate in different circumstances. The importance of assessing impact and preparing Z charts has been referred to as part of planning and acting on results. The approaches of some organisations have been referred to, which should give you an idea of the variety of methods that exist. Finally, the role of HR as a deliverer of change has been stressed, but to do this HR must be able to make a contribution that adds value through its understanding of culture and possible sources of resistance. This is the subject of Chapter 3.

3

MAPPING THE ORGANISATION

What is organisational mapping?

It is essential that having decided to embark on such a challenging project as benchmarking, or at least having contemplated the move, you have as clear an idea as possible about where you are. There are a number of issues that affect organisational performance. Figure 3 summarises the key elements. The purpose of the exercise is to analyse your present position by HR audit, survey, questionnaire, formal investigation and workshop to ensure that there is a good understanding of the present position. Is the culture working as well as you think it is? Is the reward culture conducive to a well performing organisation? Are the employees as committed to the organisation as you think they are? Have you got a trained and experienced workforce, particularly for any new challenges that lie ahead? How do you manage people? Is the general organisational style in line with what you want, or even with what the organisation needs? Are the tasks and processes organised efficiently or are you continuing with a structure that was implemented years ago in different circumstances. Finally how healthy is the company? What investment has there been? How dependent are you on a single product or source of finance? It is not just a question of profits – they may be fine for now but how vulnerable are they to a change? These are some of the questions you should consider in mapping the organisation.

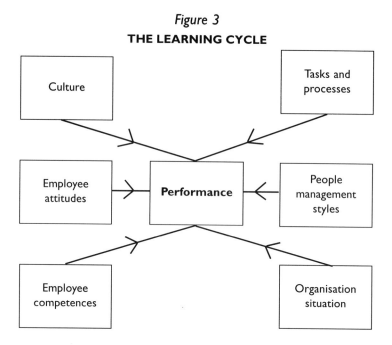

Figure 3
THE LEARNING CYCLE

What does the mapping look like?

It should be clear at the start that the metaphor of 'mapping' should not be taken to imply that you are seeking an exact replication of reality. Rather, the idea is to establish basic principles in a number of key areas. These principles interact and overlap in various ways but it is important that they are separated to make them understandable. It is possible that there are those who will argue that the exercise is not worth while because the position of the organisation and its people is well known. This argument is wrong on two counts. First, people's opinions of organisations and their reactions to them differ. One manager may believe that people are competent (and they may be), but if people feel they lack the competence to do a job (however irrational that may be) then that is a problem that needs dealing with.

The second point to be made is that one purpose of the map is to facilitate future change and development. The mapping exercise may not continue in quite the form in which it is prepared initially but some aspects of it will form a continuing programme of assessment and benchmarking for the future.

The map will be used to review and then diagnose a number of areas that impact on organisational performance. The list set out in Figure 3 may need to change, depending on the individual organisation, and you will have to decide what areas you are going to map. Some suggestions to get you started are indicated below.

Culture

This is probably the most important area. The basic task is to establish those values according to which the organisation operates. It is perhaps also useful to consider whether there is a difference between what is intended or expected, and the actual result. These are important differences. One organisation may seek to change what its stated values are because it comes to a recognition that those values run counter to what the organisation needs. However, another organisation may find that its stated values are appropriate, but they are not widely implemented – that, by and large, people do not live by them. The sorts of areas that should be studied are shown in Table 11. If you wish to develop the organisation to become more efficient and serve your customers better it is necessary to empower people and make them accountable for what they do, without resorting to blaming them for every error. It is essential that this is supported by a positive listening approach which gives employees the coaching and support they need. These are all issues that should be looked at. This exercise is not primarily about 'being a good employer' or 'being kind to employees as people' (although it is both). The purpose is to ensure that the organisation's culture helps, and does not hinder, the drive for excellence in giving customers what they want at a price they are willing to pay.

Employee attitudes

This is another important area. The problem is that employee attitude surveys have often become discredited because of a failure to act on their results. Employees quickly become cynical if the aims of an attitude survey are stated but then not met. It is very easy to believe that significant benefits and

Table 11

CULTURE MAPPING:
SOME POSSIBLE AREAS FOR INVESTIGATION

☐	Extent of empowerment, trust and 'no blame' culture.
☐	Extent of accountability.
☐	Are decisions made or avoided?
☐	Extent of use of coaching and feedback.
☐	Is the organisation achievement- and learning-oriented?
☐	Do managers or employees listen to each other?
☐	Is it an organisation that likes to say *yes*?
☐	Is the need for change accepted?
☐	Are initiatives rewarded?

changes will result – the manager is carried along by a surge of enthusiasm – but if the results fail to meet expectations then there will be a price to pay in terms of the employees' support. Every time this happens a little more emotional distance is put between the employee and the organisation. Employee support is a vital but delicate commodity.

This is an area related closely to Sid Jennings' 'Industrial Relations Audits' carried out for organisations in the 1980s (Bramham, 1994). These ideas have now been widened in scope and provide valuable information that can benchmark performance. Table 12 lists those areas of employees attitudes that should be of interest, although there will certainly be others. Such a survey can be carried out using an attitude survey, with questions being designed to reveal particular areas. Such surveys can identify a number of points, such as:

☐ positive things that employees believe
☐ those bad practices that can and should be changed quickly
☐ good things that are misunderstood and which should be explained
☐ good practices that are not applied throughout the organisation.

Table 12

MAPPING EMPLOYEE ATTITUDES: SOME POSSIBLE AREAS FOR INVESTIGATION

- ☐ Team briefings and their uses.
- ☐ Satisfaction with communications.
- ☐ Learning opportunities.
- ☐ Business development programmes.
- ☐ Reward systems and strategies.
- ☐ Development and appraisals.
- ☐ Employee relations and trade unions.
- ☐ Attendance and attitudes to its control.
- ☐ Employee benefit programmes.
- ☐ Overall view of working for this employer.

(From Sid Jennings, Oxford, quoted in Bramham, 1994.)

The exercise will help to identify the areas of strategic concern. This is really the point of such an exercise and it will need to be handled as part of a strategic view of the organisation. This is important, as there is a danger that *ad hoc* unrelated and even conflicting changes may be made. Strategy must link the various policies together and form a cohesive framework.

Employee competences

This area involves an important 'skills audit'. The idea is that competences are the skills required to do the job but cover a wider scope than many skills audits have done. The potential area is shown in Table 13. The list is divided into two sections. Some skills are important in order to be able to carry out a task satisfactorily. These will include such skills as typing, office work, engineering fitting, recruiting skills, selling, production skills, and so on. These can be called 'technical' skills, although you will find other descriptions of them. Less obviously, it is also important to be able to identify a second area of competences that can be described as 'behavioural' skills.

Table 13

MAPPING EMPLOYEE COMPETENCES:
SOME POSSIBLE AREAS FOR INVESTIGATION

Job/technical skills

- ☐ Data processing and network skills.
- ☐ Understanding of plant and equipment.
- ☐ Knowledge of the organisation.
- ☐ Supervisory and management skills.
- ☐ Professional skills (HR, law, accountancy, engineering, sales, etc).
- ☐ Qualifications (particularly those key to the organisation).

- ☐ Office skills.
- ☐ Oral skills.
- ☐ Project management.
- ☐ Written skills.

Behavioural skills

- ☐ Working in a team.
- ☐ Planning and organising.
- ☐ Initiative and performance.
- ☐ Concern for order and quality.
- ☐ Commercial and customer awareness.

- ☐ Resilience and persistence.
- ☐ Change orientation.
- ☐ Communication and listening.
- ☐ Interpersonal skills.
- ☐ Ideas orientation.

Some HR managers now rate behavioural skills as even more important than technical skills. There is some truth in a view that it is the type of person that is important to a company rather than the specific tasks that can be undertaken. Many job skills can be trained for reasonably quickly and at a cost that can be afforded. This is much less true of behavioural skills. Although it is possible for employees to change behaviour, if there is a wide range of behaviour across a large number of employees a problem will result. What can be done successfully for one person in 20 will not work so well if you have to accommodate five people in 20. There is another problem: the notion of one job and one set of skills for life is fading. Few young people believe that they will be working at the same task for 40 years until they retire. Even putting aside people's expectations for change and development in their careers, the organisation will have to change to meet new markets. The position in some privatised utilities is a case in point. In the 1970s employees must have felt certain of their future; in 1997 the companies have been changed beyond recognition.

In this environment the skills you have will become outmoded by changes in the market and in technology. The 'learning organisation' has emerged as an issue because of the need to keep up to date by continuous change and adaptation. It is hardly surprising, therefore, that the emphasis is on generic task skills training which can be adapted to meet the needs of most of the situations that will be encountered. These generic tasks have to be backed up by sound behavioural skills of the type listed in Table 13. When a car manufacturer was recruiting to establish its greenfield site factory the emphasis was initially on behavioural skills. You could be the best production worker in the world but if you objected to team-work and resisted new ideas you were no good to the company. This is even more true now than it was then. In order to change the culture a number of former nationalised industries concentrated almost exclusively on behavioural skills. Their importance can hardly be overestimated. There has to be a knowledge of people's task and behavioural competences so that potential problem areas can be assessed realistically. It may even be essential to start the benchmarking efforts in the area of competences if serious problems seem likely (Bramham 1997).

People management styles

This area can in part be derived from a survey of employee atti-tudes by asking them for their views on management in practice in the organisation. But there is likely to be a more analytical need than that. This is also a proactive matter where key competences and styles can be fashioned to meet the needs of the business. A survey of employee views on such matters is important, but like all such surveys it is only a snapshot of the perceived position at one point in time. It is important, there-fore, to keep probing such areas with various development tools such as 360-degree development, appraisals and learning workshops.

Table 14

**MAPPING MANAGEMENT STYLES:
SOME AREAS TO CONSIDER**

- ☐ Style of leadership exercised.
- ☐ Extent of empowerment and command and control.
- ☐ Extent of an open and trustworthy approach.
- ☐ Are business results important?
- ☐ Communication and feedback to employees.
- ☐ Extent to which the customer is at the centre of what we do.
- ☐ Extent to which managers care for employees.
- ☐ Is teamwork encouraged?
- ☐ Gives employees development opportunities to learn new skills.
- ☐ Likes to say yes ... will say *no*.

With management styles it is important that a proactive approach is taken throughout. The sorts of areas that might well be analysed are given in Table 14. Clearly some of the issues listed can be explored by reference to any survey of attitudes, competences and culture that takes place. However, there are also excellent frameworks that have been developed by consultants in the field. One in particular, marketed by the British Quality Foundation (BQF), has proved beneficial to many organisations, and is discussed later in this chapter.

Tasks, process and the organisation

This is an area that, when directed at the organisation's key performance drivers, is at the centre of benchmarking activity. This is not to suggest that other aspects are unimportant, but these are the key 'enablers'. By 'enablers' is meant matters that facilitate the tasks for which the business exists. The business exists to provide, for example, oil exploration, gas distribution, hospital services, policing or local authority services, and the activities of doing those tasks are the business results. The business is not there to provide 'culture' or 'good people management' – these are essential enablers to the core business. but they are not the business itself.

The enablers are

- [ ] culture
- [ ] employee attitudes
- [ ] competences
- [ ] people management styles.

These enablers also include the strategies and policies of the organisation. Strategy, policy and resources are the glue that binds together the four areas of culture, employee attitudes, competences and people management styles. Business results include such aspects as meeting customer requirements, and creating products and services that can be sold. Business results include adding value through product quality and cycle times, but they do not include the enablers of those things, however important they may be. Tasks and processes can be mapped by asking employees, customers and suppliers what they think of these various parts of the organisation in so far as they come into contact with them. What mapping tools are available to help with the benchmarking project?

Choosing a mapping tool

What will cover all the steps that it is felt should be included? The ideal should be something that is simple to use. Examples of the criteria against which to measure a prospective tool are listed in Table 15. There is no point having a tool that is heavy-handed and complex. Surveys themselves should be as short as possible and to the point. Another important issue is the extent to which you wish to compare yourself with other organisations and how you wish to achieve that. Comparing the organisation in qualitative measures is possible, but it may be better if you can achieve the exactitude that would come from numerical analysis. Metrics can be derived from the business excellence model issued by the British Quality Foundation. They are also available through proprietary questionnaires and psychometric test providers such as Oxford Psychologists 'Benchmarks'. Obviously, if you wish to use the information gained in this way for quantitative comparison it is necessary

Table 15

MAPPING THE ORGANISATION: SELECTING MAPPING TOOLS

☐ Tools should be simple to use.

☐ Consider whether you wish to use them internally or make comparisons with others.

☐ Do you want a tool that leads to discussion or focuses attention on detail?

☐ Do you want to self-assess or do you want consultant support?

☐ Look at various organisation health check models, including:

    – attitude surveys

    – psychometric models

    – SWOT analyses

    – simple pressure mapping

    – culture audits

    – business improvement models

    – HR audits and the Healthcheck.

☐ Ask consultants, advisers and other organisations what they use

    BUT ...

☐ Remember that circumstances, needs and intentions differ.

to use a proprietary tool. The use of standard questions that tend to come with such an approach can be an advantage, as it is then possible to compare results with different organisations. Of course, this limits the variability of questions as, obviously, you cannot compare your organisation with another in areas where a particular question was not asked, or was posed in a different context.

There is yet another point to consider when contemplating comparing survey results in this way. How do you know whether the 'score' that you give a particular activity means the same as when that same score is given by a different organisation? People judge such matters from different perspectives. Caution must be exercised in making comparisons of this nature. It is important to reflect carefully on the information and how it will be used. The prime purpose is to generate internal debate, and as long as any other organisation's data are used simply to give pointers it would seem to be in order. It would be inadvisable, however, to rely too heavily on such data in circumstances such as setting individual performance targets, where the risks of unreliable data could have more personal consequences. This is because of the strongly qualitative nature of such information. What is acceptable when used diagnostically across groups of managers, coaches or teams could be unsound and unfair if applied as a benchmark for individuals, particularly where there was a penalty involved for not achieving the target. In going through the sample of tools set out below, the reader will be reminded where special caution needs to be exercised. The same issue of quantitative v qualitative information to some extent bears on where you are in the benchmarking process. If the organisation is at an early stage in the process and the emphasis is on exploring some areas and perhaps building support, such tools as the excellence model and some other proprietary methods will probably be inappropriate.

It will also be necessary to consider the issues of self-assessment v externally driven assessment. In self-assessment, teams decide in a workshop setting what score they should give the organisation. This is not easy. People have to work hard to reach a consensus on what the organisation does well and what it does badly. The less expensive alternative is to ask people to rank the organisation and then analyse the scores and achieve averages in that way. Self-assessment is certainly not an easier or cheaper alternative but some would argue that the extra effort pays high dividends in terms of achieving understanding. By contrast, externally driven assessment requires interviews or questionnaires conducted by either internal or external consultants. Clearly it is not possible to get to the root of a problem by the interview and questionnaire method. Indeed, when the interview results are received the debate is only just beginning. Although perhaps not as complete in terms of analysing problems, questionnaires and interviews are usually easier and cheaper to set up.

In the end the decision has to be made by the company. Any

provider should have to explain why the service being offered is right for your organisation. The circumstances in which organisations have to manage vary considerably and the political context within the organisation is an important factor. There is no point in trying to deliver full-scale benchmarking if senior management is not supportive. If you are benchmarking in the HR department the head of the department, or at least a senior member of the team, must be fully supportive. To go beyond your own department you need still wider support. There is no point incurring significant expenditure unless there is the commitment to match.

Tools available

There are a variety of mapping tools available, all aimed at exploring the areas set out in Figure 3. As has already been explained, no single tool can be expected to cover each area neatly and completely. This is because of the inevitable overlap between the various parts. For example, in looking at process you may discover (or already be aware) that the number of 'hand – offs' or authorisation steps cause a delay in customer service offered. This results from an organisational problem that a restructuring of jobs by process management can adequately resolve. Looking again at Figure 3, each area can be considered in turn.

TOOLS – surveying employee and customer attitudes

Attitude surveys can be directed at the employee or at the customer and suppliers. The sorts of topics that can be looked at are given in Table 16. Areas such as what they think of the organisation, its quality standards, and service provided are crucial. The idea of asking employees is not new, but the suggestion that customers, or even suppliers, have a useful input to such exercises will for many be revolutionary.

What is being suggested here is that it is possible to ask questions that unearth views that will not be wholly popular. There is no point asking bland questions that do not lead anywhere. With suitably tailored questions the amount of information that can be available is extraordinary; such surveys are not shallow or ineffective in any way. An example

Table 16

SURVEYING WHAT EMPLOYEES/CUSTOMERS THINK: AREAS THAT MIGHT BE COVERED

☐ Employees' and customers' view of the organisation.

☐ Teamwork.

☐ Quality and customer service.

☐ Development and learning opportunities.

☐ Communication and listening.

☐ Openness of managers.

☐ What is rewarded?

☐ Are status issues a barrier?

☐ Are employee representational or union arrangements good?

☐ Is the organisation unnecessarily bureaucratic?

☐ Are business issues high up the organisation agenda at all levels?

of an attitude survey report is given in Figure 4. It is possible to ask employees the same question as is asked in other organisations. In this way it is possible to compare yourself with the performance of others. The problem is that the meaning of the questions will vary from company to company. The advantage is that, by adopting this approach, external benchmarks can be set and then worked towards. Whatever approach is used, by repeating the questions in subsequent surveys carried out regularly (but not too frequently) it is possible to map the organisation's progress over time.

TOOLS – analysing people management styles

The guiding behaviours indicated in Table 17 can be investigated in teams or directly through an individual questionnaire using a '360-degree' approach (also called 4-way feedback or multifeedback). This is simply a method of getting assessments from subordinates, peers, boss and customers on an individual's performance – that is, views from all the people who work around you, hence 360 degrees. The way people approach the job of managing is important to how the

Figure 4
SURVEYING WHAT EMPLOYEES AND CUSTOMERS THINK: EXAMPLE OF SURVEY REPORT

Communications

How satisfied are you with communications within the company?

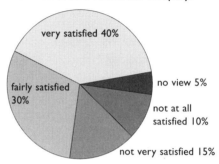

(N=1,150)

As the above chart shows, seven in ten of our respondents are at least fairly satisfied with communications within the company.

However, as the breakdown table below shows, those who have worked for the company for a longer period of time are more likely to be satisfied.

	Length of service				
	Up to 1 year N=462 (%)	1–5 years N=343 (%)	5–10 years N=179 (%)	10–15 years N=108 (%)	15 years or more N=58
Very satisfied	9.5	11.9	29.6	47.3	52
Fairly satisfied	15.1	15.5	27.2	32.5	3
Not very satisfied	23.4	19.3	17.7	15.7	3
Not at all satisfied	28.8	25.6	16.1	2.9	–
No view	23.2	27.7	9.4	1.6	–

In this table, numbers rather than percentages are used for groups from which fewer than 100 responses were received.

Of those respondents who are employed on a part-time basis, 85.9% said that they are satisfied with communications. This compares with 64.7% of full-timers.

Table 17

ANALYSING EMPLOYEE ATTITUDES:
TEAMWORK – EXAMPLES OF GUIDING BEHAVIOURS

☐ Acts for the long-term benefit of the company even when it may detract from short-term personal benefit.

☐ Develops positive working relationships with peers and others.

☐ Supports team-mates to succeed.

☐ Involves others in discussing issues and resolving conflicts.

☐ Acknowledges others who demonstrate teamwork.

☐ Informs and involves team-mates whenever possible.

☐ Seeks win/win solutions.

☐ Shares information and resources with others.

☐ Gives credits to others for their contributions.

organisation performs. It is essential to be able to identify problems with any styles that emerge.

Examples of models based on the 360-degree framework approach are providing the opportunity to establish benchmarks of performance. For example, after investigating performance (and perhaps backed up by surveys) it may become apparent that managers do not listen to or communicate with staff. The 360-degree process will confirm this finding – by asking people questions about management styles. If listening communication is indeed a problem then steps can be taken to consider that matter. In benchmarking terms, a good internal department (or perhaps an external user) can be used to establish the benchmark and – thus the scale of improvement required. Such techniques used in this way to create benchmarks of good performance are a new approach to an old problem. Of course, the data must be used with some caution. It would be wrong to focus rewards on too narrow a band of data derived in this way. It may be better to aggregate results and establish an organisation-wide benchmark for communication. In this way any arbitrary results can be averaged out. Such techniques are particularly useful in identifying employee's strengths and weaknesses. They can provide valuable insights into employee's abilities to meet crises or handle major projects. Such feedback instruments are generally used for employee development purposes but they also have a value in benchmarking. For example, the extent to which teamwork is a preferred style is important and can be explored using techniques designed for a different purpose, but having a benchmarking application.

TOOLS – undertaking a SWOT analysis

The swot analysis, a definition of which is shown in Table 18, is a well-known model designed to assess strengths and weaknesses, opportunities and threats that exist within an organisation or department. This latter point is important. Such an exercise may be carried out on behalf of the whole company, but the possibility of restricting issues to one department should not be ignored – particularly if the support of other departments has not been obtained.

The tool can be used as a general model for stimulating discussion and starting a process for diagnosing problems and their possible solutions. In a SWOT analysis the four basic categories are turned into questions and people are asked to complete a questionnaire or attend a workshop. Figure 5 shows the result of a SWOT analysis undertaken at an HR department workshop preview of its activities. This sort of informal study has been around for a long time as a tool for assessing organisations. The advantage is that it can be obtained, for

Table 18
SWOT ANALYSIS

Strengths	– What are you good at?
Weaknesses	– Where are the key problem areas?
Opportunities	– What challenges lie ahead for growth?
	Are you geared up to grasp them?
Threats	– What issues lie ahead that might derail you?
	– How far ahead are they?

Figure 5
SWOT ANALYSIS FOR AN HR DEPARTMENT:
MAPPING PRESSURE POINTS

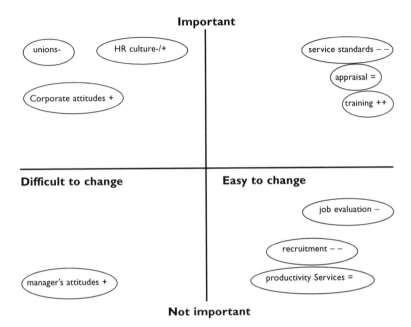

Important

unions-   HR culture-/+

service standards − −

appraisal =

Corporate attitudes +

training ++

Difficult to change   **Easy to change**

job evaluation −

recruitment − −

productivity Services =

manager's attitudes +

Not important

Key:
+ or − indicates getting better or worse (from one to three indicates degree)
= is neither good nor bad

From Templeton College, Oxford University

example, during structured training sessions. It is not necessary to undertake extensive surveys to be able to make some progress.

More recently, however, proprietary approaches have been adopted which bring some discipline into such techniques. SWOTCheck is one such tool that is available and which should be investigated. The SWOTCheck has been developed by the Ward Dutton Partnership, with others. It is designed to improve the structure and flow of information. Like traditional surveys, it is based on an assumption that employees have analytical skills and, especially when taken together, they can provide useful pointers to how the organisation should progress and what its problems might be. The exercise is data-driven, unlike the example in Figure 5. However, the model is computer-based, which greatly facilitates collection and analysis of data. The questioning process can be handled by either internal interviewers, direct 'self-assessment' or can be consultant supported. Contact points are given in the Appendix 2 at the end of this book.

TOOLS – undertaking an audit of culture

It is important that a review is undertaken of the culture and the related value systems within the organisation. Again, the approach can be to ask teams in groups or as individuals what is their view of the organisation, what are the perceived cultural strengths, and what impact will they have on benchmarking. You may find that people value tradition and the support given to employees, but you may wonder whether benchmarking will raise the question of whether those practices can be afforded. At the same time employees may believe that a cultural weakness is an inability to innovate. This may just be the 'flip side' of a respect for tradition, but if the organisation cannot adopt new ideas it will have a considerable impact on the benchmarking project.

An example exercise is shown in Table 19, although this is part of a whole battery of such approaches directed at changing culture as part of a long-term programme. This can be a useful aid to facilitate discussion and to get employees to challenge their culture and value systems. There is one word of caution that should be mentioned: what one organisation (especially in a different national culture) may regard as a strength, another organisation may regard as a weakness. It is therefore essential that a view is developed about what the department or organisation needs before proceeding too far on such an investigation. There is also the issue of which areas of culture are important for your particular organisation at a particular time. An HR department that has employee and union relationships that are going off the rails will have quite different (and possibly jaundiced) views about the cultural importance of talking to employees and their representatives than one where constructive relations exist.

If there is reason to believe that significant changes have to be made to the culture of the organisation it may be necessary

Table 19

CULTURE AND BENCHMARKING

List the key strengths and weaknesses of your current culture. Talk through with your team the issues and implications these can have for benchmarking.

Cultural strengths	**Impact on benchmarking**
Key areas:	
Less key areas:	

Cultural weaknesses	**Impact on benchmarking**
Key areas:	
Less key areas:	

to regard this area as such a major one that it will eclipse all others. If it is apparent that other issues are more important then the effort and expertise involved in culture change can be put to one side. Of course, this refers to a special culture change programme. Culture is an integral part of everything that is done and will be affected to a greater or lesser extent by all the changes that are entered into in benchmarking.

TOOLS – the business excellence model

The BQF business excellence model shown in Figure 6 provides a good tool for mapping the organisation. Although requiring an extensive time commitment, it is a simple and straight-forward tool which, when repeated, provides a regular snapshot of change within an organisation. In this way the results from regular snapshots can be used to compare the organisation's progress with its own results over time. Aspects that attract many organisations to this model are its comprehensive nature and the ability to be able to establish benchmarks of perfor-mance with other users. It provides an organisation with key benchmarks that can be used for tracking progress under the various headings.

The model sets out the three areas of people, policy and resources that are crucial to an organisation's success. The model was developed in the 1980s by leading European busi-nesses in order to increase the awareness and acceptance of quality as an issue. It was part of that emerging recognition of customers and quality, backed by a recognition of the funda-mental importance of people in delivering an excellent and successful company. The nine areas of the business environ-ment are involved. For example, a major utility facing massive change placed these in a matrix to facilitate self-assessment, as shown in Table 20.

Organisations that engage in this exercise have a variety of approaches available to them. They can use a questionnaire which can either be one provided by the BQF or developed in-house from a BQF model. It is also possible to use a matrix of the type shown in Table 20 which, although excellent for getting to the issues can for many organisations be too time-consuming. A compromise is to carry out the assessment using a workshop approach which can then be as long or as short as

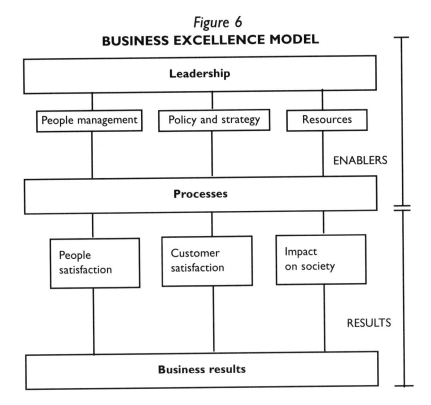

Figure 6
BUSINESS EXCELLENCE MODEL

you require. All of these choices will be affected by the time that can be allocated to the project and this in turn will be affected by the extent of senior management commitment. The five enablers and four key result areas are given below, with short definitions of what is meant by each.

1   Leadership – how the executive team and all managers behave to inspire and drive the culture change towards a high-quality organisation.

2   Policy and strategy – how the company's policy and strategy reflect the commitment and drive towards continuous improvement in the business.

3   People management – how the company manages its resources and releases the full potential of its people.

4   Resources – how the key financial, information, application of technology and material resources are effectively

managed and utilised to support the organisation's policy and strategy.

5   Processes – how the key processes of the business unit are identified, reviewed and revised to create an environment of continuous improvement within the organisation.

The four key results areas are concerned with how the unit measures its performance. They occur as a result of the development of the change in business philosophy.

A   Customer satisfaction – what is the perception of the unit's customers regarding the provision of products and services?

B   People satisfaction – what do the employees of the unit feel about the organisation?

C   Impact on society – what is the perception of the company among society at large in terms of quality of life, the environment, preservation of resources, and involvement in the community?

D   Business results – what is the unit achieving relative to its planned business performance?

The foregoing definitions provide the column headings for Table 20. Under each of these nine headings the business or department is assessed as being in one of ten categories to determine its position on the scale. These statements are too lengthy to be reproduced in this book for each of the ten categories. However, as an example, one set of definitions is given in Table 21 for one of the axes, which in this case is 'people management.' In this example the scale of people management routines varies from basic at no. 1 to empowerment and the learning organisation at no. 10. Once a score has been identified by self-assessment or by survey, it can then be compared with what other organisations achieve, and a benchmark determined. Steps can then be put in place to improve the weak areas so that when the exercise is repeated in the future the extent of advance can be determined. Organisations can submit themselves for European Quality Awards (EQA) which is based on a scoring mechanism using this model available from the BQF. The use of this award to encourage excellence is not unlike the Baldridge Award or the Deming Award in the

Table 20

BUSINESS IMPROVEMENT MATRIX

STEP	Leadership	Policy and strategy	People manage- ment	Resources	Processes	Customer satisfaction	People satisfaction	Impact on society	Business results
10									
9									
8									
7						▓			▓
6									
5		▓							
4	▓			▓					
3			▓		▓				
2							▓	▓	
1									

Method

Teams assess each statement and decide which applies to their department and/or organisation. The detailed statements for one column (people management) are given in Table 21. When a consensus is reached, the square is shaded. Different colours can be used where the step is partially achieved.

If a survey or questionnaire approach is used, the team results are averaged to identify which square should be shaded.

After the exercise, actions to improve performance can be identified. Improvement steps to identify expected future achievement can be set out.

Notice the similarity of these indicators to a balanced scorecard approach.

Reproduced with permission of the British Quality Foundation.

Table 21

BUSINESS EXCELLENCE MODEL: PEOPLE MANAGEMENT

How you manage resources and release the full potential of your people

10 All employees are regularly appraised and their training needs revised as a result of their appraisal. All training and development activity is evaluated in terms of its effectiveness. There is an environment where all employees are encouraged to form improvement groups and are empowered to act on their suggestions.

9 There is evidence that employees are empowered to use their judgement and make decisions in most situations concerning the day-to-day running of the processes in which they are involved. There is a formal system giving clear parameters which identify situations when further guidance should be sought. This system covers all of the anticipated decisions needed on a day-to-day basis. Employees are making business improvements in their workplace.

8 A Human Resource Plan containing future plans for recruitment, development and promotion is in place. To colour this box, the Human Resource Plan must also contain elements which value, recognise and support participation in continuous improvement within day-to-day operations.

7 There are well-used/well-established processes in place to capture and encourage the natural creativity and innovation of employees. In-house facilities and processes are used to capture ideas and implement them. Employees feel empowered to make changes in their work environment.

6 Improvement teams are created and encouraged to identify opportunities for improvement of business performance. The teams and their champions receive adequate support to enable them to produce useful recommendations which can be implemented. Teams are encouraged to implement recommendations with the assistance/support of their management team, as a start towards an empowered workforce.

5 A structured process is in place to define the skills needed for the job and to assess whether the employees possess skills. These skill gap evaluations, along with the personal and business aims identified in Step 4 are then used to develop and revise plans for the training and development of all employees.

4 All employees within the unit receive regular appraisals of performance. People should be able to conduct them in a systematic and professional manner to build credibility and establish comparable trends of performance. Appraisals should encompass the needs of both the organisation and the individual.

3 There is a method in place to select and effectively communicate relevant business information to employees. There is an environment which encourages bottom-up communication from employees without fear of reprisal.

2 The unit has openly declared its intention to provide the necessary resources for developing all employees to ensure that its business goals can be achieved. An example of this type of commitment would be Investors in People.

1 A method exists for collecting employee opinions and then tracking those opinions over time.

From material provided through the good offices of the British Quality Foundation

United States and Japan. One problem is that the submission process is very extensive, and definitely not for the unprepared or the faint-hearted. As always, you are recommended to start off with a simple approach and later consider progressing to something perhaps more fulfilling but more resource-hungry.

TOOLS – other tools for HR benchmarking

As organisations recognise and confirm that people are a key to competitive advantage, it is becoming increasingly important to make the best use of the investment in the 'people assets'. At a time of globalisation, competition and rapid change you must make sure that people issues are at the top of the business agenda so that the changes can be managed effectively.

Of course, you should look to benchmark key people policies and people processes against what other organisations are doing. You will be looking to benchmark, for example:

☐ key workforce metrics (such as age analysis, length of service, employee competences, absenteeism, balance between value-adding, asset-adding employees, etc)

☐ the current focus of the HR resources against the main HR processes

☐ the size of the HR function in relation to the size of the business

☐ HR policies for reward, development, learning, change management, employee relations, teamwork and communications

☐ HR-related business issues that need to be focused on now.

What is at issue is trying to find out where your company is now. What state are you in? What problems are likely to emerge in the near future? What are your value systems and do they differ from what you expect and what might be needed in the future? In a period of rapid change it is important that these and other issues have been thought through. It is essential that this is done anyway (and most of these tools and techniques can be used successfully independently of any benchmarking exercise) but it is particularly important if the organisation intends to introduce benchmarking against top-class companies. This process can help the debate on the activities, role, size, and general strategic thrust of the HR function. This is particularly important for those organisations undergoing significant growth or contraction, or going through other changes. All these matters interrelate and a change in one area can often be achieved only if there is a change in another.

This is part of the consulting approach offered by such organisations as Coopers & Lybrand and Pilat, aimed at raising standards in HR through auditing and measuring HR activities. Both have HR tools and approaches where benchmarking helps organisations to determine the people issues facing them and to act upon them. Some of the specific issues have been referred to above, to which must be added ensuring that HR systems and technology meet the organisation's needs. Above all the process provides an external perspective on how well organisations perform in their management of people. There are many other organisations apart from those mentioned as examples. It is rather like having a healthcheck or MOT of the HR department. There is so much available – go and find what suits you and make use of it.

Summary and conclusion

This chapter has been directed towards showing how an organisation can get a realistic assessment of where it stands across the whole HR and business field. The areas of culture, employee attitudes, competences, management styles, and tasks and processes have been discussed. The tools that are available include surveys and questionnaires, 360-degree approaches to understanding how people's performance is seen, SWOT analyses, cultural audits, HR audits and healthchecks and the business excellence model. It should be taken as read that before you can move forward purposefully you must have a clear idea of where you are. This chapter will help you do just that.

4

CULTURE, VALUES AND PEOPLE

Culture and benchmarking

Any change programme is dependent for its success on the culture in which it operates. In this book the word 'values' is preferred to 'culture'. 'Values' does not have the political connotations of 'culture'. It seems reasonable to suggest that employees can, to a point, suspend their own values and beliefs and 'buy-into' the values of the organisation in which they are working at a particular time. As long as there is not inconsistency between the person's cultural beliefs and the organisation's requirements this arrangement can work well. The closer the organisation's values are to the employee's national cultural values the easier any assimilation will be and the stronger will be the result. It is a fundamental prerequisite that in order to implement benchmarking successfully you must look at culture and understand the problems and opportunities that may result. This chapter will do more than consider values – it will suggest what sort of culture will facilitate the introduction of benchmarking, and with it the innovative, customer-driven, learning organisation appropriate for the future.

Culture cannot be proclaimed

It is important to understand what *cannot* be done. Values cannot be changed by simply repeating the articles of faith. What is important is actions. What is the point of saying 'this organisation rewards excellence' when everyone can see that all employees receive virtually the same pay increases regardless of contribution? Or 'this is a learning organisation' when the reality is that people have little opportunity to expand their knowledge and employees see that training is the first casualty of any budget cuts? Then again, people who hear managers proclaim that 'our employees are our most valuable asset', are naturally cynical when they see the organisation 'downsizing' or 'outsourcing' their jobs, so their pay and conditions can be cut. Even the language of downsizing and outsourcing is intended to conceal and soften what is really being done – making people redundant.

This is the difference between 'stated' policy and 'done' policy. People look not at what is said but at what is done. Managers often say that no one listens to them. In fact employees listen very carefully! Employees know that when you say you have 20 priorities the reality is you have none. This is, of course, a problem for the MD or CEO. Employees watch carefully and any analysis of values has to start with the values of top executives. It is actions, not words, that count.

The need for change

What are the important values that are an integral part of benchmarking? The most important is perhaps a recognition of a need to change – change that will be relentless; change that will continue even when you are the best. Benchmarking may indeed show that in some key areas your company is flying high, but the need for change remains. It is not a case of getting through this major change operation and then everything will be calm. The days of plain sailing through calm waters have long gone.

An organisation adopts benchmarking for a variety of reasons; it continues benchmarking for only one reason – it recognises the need to change. This will be change that embraces the incremental, continuous change inherent in total quality management. But there is also something else. Much of the change that will be required will be step change that enables the organisation not only to catch up with, but to outpace its competitors. This is the important message of the Z chart referred to in Chapter 2. If benchmarking analysis shows up a gap in performance it is essential to bridge that gap quickly.

This is a change process that is permanent. There will be no slack periods interspersed by frenetic activity. There will be continual change and a constant search for it. Benchmarking will be visited and revisited. Far from having employees who are distressed by change we should be seeking a culture where people feel unhappy and insecure when nothing is changing! People should see the *status quo* for what it is – complacency, decline and the end of their organisation. Change enables them and their families to stay in jobs. This is the biggest cultural change of all and it will take time to achieve. It is not caused by benchmarking, but benchmarking requires it for success and it is one of its driving forces.

NIH: The 'not invented here' syndrome

The resistance to change from 'outside' is strong. The suggestion that there is something that can be learnt damages our pride and reduces our view of ourselves. But this is not only an important barrier to change generally – it is absolutely counter to the idea of benchmarking. If there is any suggestion of the NIH syndrome in the organisation, this has to be dealt with before any progress can be made on a wide scale.

There is a problem here, particularly if benchmarking is forced on an unwilling department or organisation. If there is no support for what is being presented the benchmarking results will meet with fierce criticism. The prognosis is familiar. Managers criticise every stage of the process; items are sent to committees for consideration; proposals are held over pending some major event; there will be explanation as to why the metrics are not relevant; there will be argument that they are misleading. Every error or inconsistency will be seized upon with great enthusiasm and will be used to discredit the whole. Benchmarking requires a value system that has as one of its main feature a willingness to learn from others. There has to be this acceptance for benchmarking to function properly.

Preparedness to take initiatives

Benchmarking can lead to measures that show that your organisation is falling behind in innovation, costs and efficiency. How can such problems be overcome? Benchmarking is unlikely to establish a clear 'one shot' solution. Employees have to show a willingness to take initiatives – to act to try to improve the business. People should be encouraged to develop ideas in their own area in order to reduce costs, improve cycle times, and enhance product and service quality. Many organisations find this very difficult to put into practice. 'People will get things wrong and only I know the whole story' is the view of many managers. But of course the situation on the job is changing radically.

First, cost reductions often mean reducing the numbers of employees and as a result having fewer managers to whom employees can defer to take business decisions. Managers of the past, in their old hierarchies supported by innumerable staff, have been 'de-layered' and 'downsized'. Even if a manager has a desire to take all the decisions the span of control exercised in the job would not allow it. The second issue is that employees have to be given responsibility to take decisions because otherwise they cannot respond quickly and meaningfully to customers' requests. An organisation that requires any change to be approved by a complex managerial structure will be too slow, will stagnate and will eventually atrophy. It is essential that a stated value is one where people take the initiative within their competence to make decisions. This is what is needed for benchmarking to be a success.

There will be exceptions to this. Employees, like organisations, are constrained by legal and codes of practice requirements. These will be driven by external bodies (government and professional bodies and other agencies) and internally set standards and policies. No one is suggesting that freedom to take initiatives implies a licence to do as you please! What is being suggested is that even within the normal boundaries of what can be done, there is scope for people to be allowed greater responsibility for making decisions in their own jobs – to allow greater empowerment of people in their jobs.

Risk-taking as a way of working

Related to a desire that employees should take initiatives is a recognition that this will also involve risk-taking. The problem is that if employees always avoid the possibility of making mistakes they will always 'play safe'. There will be occasions where that is a sensible strategy to follow. Some areas of the organisation will include work in which risks cannot be taken, though these are fewer than might be thought. In benchmarking you will be faced with uncertainties. In order to change from established practices a degree of risk is inevitable. The outcome of a changed process will be unclear and mistakes will be made. In the context of benchmarking, the organisation may well decide that risk-taking is a desirable value. The problem is that if risks are not taken, employees' ability to adapt methods that they have seen elsewhere is hampered. It is not possible to take initiatives and to implement change without an element of risk-taking. This is because it is often not possible to foresee the consequences.

A 'No-blame' organisation

Benchmarking will identify many areas for change. To facilitate the consequential changes you have will seek to establish values to avoid 'NIH' and encourage initiative, and risk- and decision-taking. But these must be supported by removing the fear of blame. The pointing finger is the sign that something has gone wrong, so everyone runs for cover. It is possible that the fear of blame stifles initiative and growth more than anything else – all the more so if the person feels that he or she has done nothing wrong. It has often been said that a person who does not make mistakes does not make anything. It has to be taken as read that no change can be brought about with perfection. Errors will occur. The organisation's response to those errors is crucial. An overcritical response will stifle and perhaps kill further change responses. People can make mistakes that to wiser heads (but usually to those having the benefit of hindsight) seem stupid and avoidable. The manager who has to take responsibility without the satisfaction of having someone to blame can be in a very uncomfortable situation. Blaming people makes the person criticising feel good, and those hearing the blame being handed out (as long as they are not involved) feel doubly satisfied. In such situations no one thinks of the damaging effect on the confidence of the individual being blamed.

From a cultural viewpoint there is a more insidious effect on the large numbers of employees who are not involved but who are wondering about their own situation and musing 'There, but for the grace of God, go I.' All these people will be a little more cautious in the future. That should not surprise us. Examples are made of those who commit mistakes, for the purpose of frightening others in the vicinity. The greater the impact that can be made, the more widely the incident will be spoken of. As Voltaire once famously remarked, some think that it is a good thing to shoot an admiral now and then *pour encourager les autres* – 'to encourage the others'.

The important point to think through is whether the person knew, or should have known, what the consequences would be. Was the employee going against a clear policy? Had the mistake been committed before? The manager and employees will have to be realistic. There are some jobs and some mistakes that it can be difficult to be relaxed about. But if this is accepted then the damaging effects of a heavy blame culture on the people who work for the organisation must also be recognised. Far better to assume a 'no-blame' value system and deal with exceptions, rather than to have employees assuming that any error will lead to retribution.

Finally, any suggestion that a no-blame value system is a soft option can be dismissed immediately. Any errors (as well as successes) should be investigated. People should have to account for their behaviour and show how they have learnt from it. Mistakes will make people uncomfortable but it is important that they feel supported throughout, and not exposed.

Making decisions

It may seem unnecessary to put this as a suggestion to managers. All managers take decisions and all employees take decisions in the areas for which they are responsible. But do they? Are not some organisations typified by a desire to pass decisions up the managerial hierarchy? The 'hand-offs' routine is common in many departments. Some small query is found on some issue in a report, which is then returned (through the internal post to slow everything down still further!) to the report writer. In this way a decision is put off. A more institutionalised form of the same idea is the committee. Committees are an invention for the prevention of decision-taking. If by chance a decision is made, the second defensive feature of committees comes into play. Because there are so many people round the table no one is to blame if anything goes wrong.

Even the best organisations play these games to some extent. Personal ambition and the desire for advancement create the uncertain circumstances in which suspicion and doubt thrive. What is being suggested is that a value system be stated as policy and lived through in actions where decisions are made and not passed on. Of course, problems will exist but they can be radically reduced. If the organisation is expected to react quickly to circumstances then people must take decisions. It must not be thought that this is directed only at managers. All employees must take decisions within their area of work. People must understand that the reassurance of referring items to others is not necessary.

Support for learning

This is an area where the value system of many organisations is contrary to what modern competitive circumstances require. It certainly does not mean that employees can go on any training course that takes their fancy. It is partly about training, but also about an acceptance that it is possible to learn from anyone – not just from those higher up the organisation! It is probable that benchmarking in reducing authority steps, cutting out hand-offs and improving efficiency, and so on, will lead to employees having to learn to do many jobs in new ways. Training has to be a core value if the organisation is to deliver the change.

There is something else, though. It is how information is passed on within the organisation so that the same mistakes are not made again. In this way the organisation has systems and processes set up in such a way that learning is efficient and knowledge is immediately transmitted to all other units that might be able to make use of it. Learning should be a continuous and frequent experience that is part of a person's work and not separate from it. It should always provide the opportunity to reflect on the organisation's values and bring employees ever closer to them.

Coaching and support

Related to learning is the value that is given to the support of employees and managers as they seek to implement a benchmarking programme. Are employees left to struggle alone or are they to be coached and helped? How can employees learn from mistakes and successes if the support systems do not exist? An organisation that does not give time for sharing other department's successes will not get those successes passed on throughout the organisation.

It has been said that much of organisational life is over-managed and underled (Peters and Waterman 1982). If that is so, the move to coaches and leaders rather than managers and controllers is being given a significant push by other, often financial, pressures on organisations. Many firms have to make changes in this and other areas when they undertake benchmarking and discover that successful firms are increasingly being managed in this way. It is important to reflect that it is not possible to pick up only bits of a successful organisation. It is often necessary to adapt some parts of the infrastructure at the same time – in other words, the cultural support that the organisation gives to that process.

Command and control

The innovation and change that is the mark of successful benchmarking will work less effectively in a 'command and control' environment. An organisation that relies on company discipline rather than company spirit cannot expect to get the full support of the people it employs. There is an illusion that somehow a perfect organisation can be constructed; that there is a universal right way of doing things. There is no one way of doing such things. The furious pace of product change, along with demanding customers and limited resources, means that adaptation has to be the way to proceed. The fact is that too many controls, too much management and supervision will stifle people on the ground with the job to do.

Command and control leads to employees who feel restricted and bored instead of free and enthusiastic.

If you intend to challenge organisational values such as 'not invented here', shunning of change, refusal to take initiatives, and so on, the area of command and control must be considered. As has already been stated, some controls are always necessary. The organisation cannot allow employees licence to do as they please. Some organisations (the police force is an example) and some parts of organisations (such as surgical operations or nuclear power) require a clear and controlled environment. Experimentation is not to be the order of the day when undertaking life-threatening medical operations, processing uranium or dealing with civil disorder. The issue, therefore, is how much can sensibly be done to remove the restrictions and bureaucracy and give people power to make changes that benchmarking with other organisations will show is successful.

Teamworking

The driving force for teamworking is the need to improve quality. The flatter, less managed, structures that have come about either through design or cost-cutting (or both) have been picked up by organisations comparing themselves through benchmarking. Employees were grouped around business processes that could be production or service based. Tasks to be done over a period are handed by the manager to the team leader, who then looks to the team to complete the tasks in the most appropriate manner. There are some potential problems with introducing teamworking. One survey, for example (LRD Survey 1995), found that shop stewards believe that the opportunity for them to talk to their members is severely reduced. There is also the possibility that an employee may grumble about the work being allocated by the team of which the employee is part. In the past the employee might complain to the union and the union might pursue the complaint with management. Teamworking driven by benchmarking processes does not have responsibility placed so neatly and conveniently. The employee is part of the team that made the decision and the organisation may reasonably say that any problem has to be handled at that level. This must be the way benchmarking is implemented. While the general structure of a programme can be decided by managers, employees in teams must be trusted to deal with the inevitable day-to-day problems that arise.

Implementing strategic vision of culture and values

This chapter has listed key issues that must be looked at as part of a review of culture. The point on which to be clear is that benchmarking cannot be undertaken like a shopping trip. You cannot have a little empowerment and a bit of initiative-taking! Even less can you expect to cherry-pick methods and processes without also looking at the cultural infrastructure that supports the organisation being benchmarked. Such an approach will not work. A strategic approach in which all items are linked and in balance is the ideal, as represented in Figure 7 and discussed again below.

The items that have been looked at in this chapter that are listed in Table 22 are not in their entirety essential for bench-marking to take place. It is possible to implement some low-level benchmarking without changing value systems at all. What is being suggested is that these are the sort of issues that are being looked at by organisations that are successfully reinventing how they work. You will find that the bigger the issues that arise in your benchmarking programme and the greater the extent of change you are looking for, the more you will be compelled to look at your organisation's values.

How can such matters be introduced? It is very important that the list of items in Table 22 is not simply worked through as a check-list with additions and deletions that meet a manager's particular fancy. First, a statement of the organisa-tion's vision is important and a set of core values and behaviours that underpin them is vital. This can be worked on and passed to people for comment. However, if those messages are unclear or conflict in any way, if the obvious is missed or (for equally obvious reasons) if there is not overriding focus and intent, the programme will not succeed. So you must establish a set of values and set out any differences from your present

Figure 7
A BALANCED STRATEGY
FOR A HIGH-PERFORMANCE CULTURE

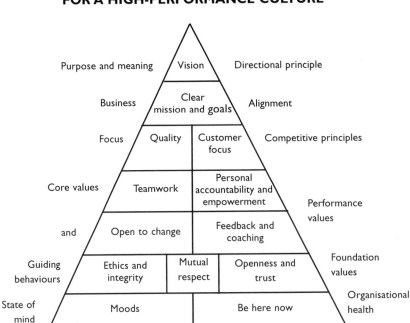

values. You should be aiming for a list of the type set out in Chapter 10, Table 43.

You must then give employees a clear path to follow and they must know how they are expected to behave. If your organisation is bureaucratic you must free up employees and set up working groups to recommend reducing hand-offs and authorisation steps. You can facilitate this by having employees from all levels of the organisation and different departments involved. In this way teamwork, empowerment, and initiative-taking will all grow. There is no other way to change culture than by attending to detail in this way. You can proclaim these values at a major conference backed up by team briefings and the like. But do not forget that you will be judged by what you *do*, not what you proclaim at some set-piece conference. Such a statement must include all those aspects

Table 22

CULTURE AND VALUES

☐	Accepting the need for change.
☐	Getting rid of *not invented here*.
☐	Preparedness to take initiatives.
☐	Risk-taking as a way of working.
☐	A 'no-blame' culture.
☐	Make decisions; avoid hand-offs.
☐	Remove or reduce authorisation steps.
☐	Build a learning and supporting organisation.
☐	Limiting command and control.
☐	Encourage teamworking, not just individual effort.
☐	Empowered, trusted and enabled employees.
☐	Get social values right.

of leadership, goals, missions, quality and customer focus that have been the subject of this chapter. Coaching and feedback and an openness to change, along with integrity and trust, are important. You must note the results from your mapping surveys about what employees think about coaching and support, and act on it. But it is also important that these values are closely related to the organisation's customers. The customer focus you need is consistent with the values described in this chapter. Social values referred to in Table 22 are also important. An organisation that treats one group of employees unfairly will do the same to another when the circumstances suit. Employees understand the messages from such values. Values are not something separate that you can have or not have as the mood takes you. Whatever they are, and even if they conflict, your organisation has values – and employees work within them. If there is no strategic integration of business values with how people are treated you cannot expect a positive response from employees. There is a foundation to these values in that if you want employees to be 'switched on', to be 'here now', you must treat them with respect and integrity. This is the message set out in Figure 7 which shows a model of a high-performance culture that will be well able to cope with the inevitable change that bench-marking will show is necessary. Starting at the bottom of Figure 7 is the recognition that what people *feel* is crucial to behaviour, and thus to organisational health. This leads on to ethical considerations of openness and trust. With these in place it is possible to develop empowerment, teamwork and a willingness to accept change. At the top of the figure are the vision and goals that are essential to providing a high quality service to customers.

Senior executives must understand the new value system and be given their own workshop on what it means in practice. This should be backed up by asking employees, trade unions and other stakeholders what the values mean to them. Extending the employee surveys used in organisational mapping is an excellent way of achieving the recognition that these ideas will require. In this way, employees can be asked what their experience of the new values is in practice. The business excellence approach described in Chapter 3 is a good way of finding out whether your actions are meeting your aspi-rations. The point to register is that, as Figure 7 implies, you cannot have a bit of trust and a high quality product without having in place the other items as well. Of course, as presented here this is an ideal, but if you have many aspects working on the opposite side, as shown in Table 43, the result will not be what you intend.

Summary and conclusion

This chapter has encouraged the discussion of culture and values. Unless values of the type discussed here are introduced as part of an integrated business strategy, benchmarking will not fulfil its promise and may well fail. The chances of failure will be related to the extent to which the organisation has value on the 'wrong' side of Table 43 and the extent of change expected from benchmarking. Finally, all these changes must be translated into actions. It is insufficient to proclaim a 'no blame', risk-taking, innovative learning organisation, while continuing with values that are more at home in command and control structures. There is no easy way of implementing a changed value system. It must be identified and then the values lived in practice at every opportunity.

5

PROCESS ORGANISATIONS

Process and benchmarking

Process is a fundamental concept that underpins benchmarking. A process is what people do, and in the final analysis this is what will have to be looked at. A process organisation is one where hand-offs and authorisation steps are reduced to a minimum by organising work around the process. This is what this chapter is about. We are all familiar with company reorganisations that seem to achieve little. There are many reasons for this, but one of them is because it may be processes, not structure, that is at fault. Changing the structure without looking at process issues can leave the problem unresolved. You cannot change the organisation fundamentally by only manipulating its structure. It is also necessary to understand the processes and go on from there to identify the core processes that really drive the organisation.

The danger with first-level benchmarking is that you may know a lot about costs and performance and how you compare with other organisations. Your profit, return on assets, capital base, employment costs and number of employees are all pertinent matters to benchmark and can be reasonably easy to get at for your own organisation and from competitors. In service organisations there is a host of metrics being collected that cast light on the relative value of the service being provided. The number of nurses in hospitals, number of operations and length of delay before seeing a consultant and, of course, the numerous statistics collected on costs. In education and local government there are many statistics that give information about how well an organisation is doing. It is rarely possible to stop there; further analysis of the underlying process will usually yield interesting results.

Unfocused 'downsizing'

The raw metrics of profit, cost, performance, number of employees, productivity or whatever, do not throw much light on what should be done to deal with the problem. For example, the benchmarking analysis may show that the organisation has higher costs and is employing more people than its competitors. The problem comes when someone issues a 'downsizing' order so that costs are reduced by making employees redundant. When budget cutting is done arbitrarily it leaves untouched all the problems that led to the cost problem in the first place. The complicated procedures, the faults in production, the high call-back rate in service, the lengthy delivery times, the failure in stores and provisioning that leads to wasted visits by employees to customers waiting on service visits. In HR terms such issues would be the bureaucratic procedures, the ineffective training, the non-existent development schemes, the mistargeted rewards – unless these areas are reviewed and problems identified, successful change will be unlikely. The downsizing exercise will, no doubt, catch some waste and lead to the removal of some unnecessary activities. However, on the whole 'cutting' manpower and budgets in such an arbitrary way does not solve the underlying problems. It may even make them worse. It does so by forcing cuts across the board, and therefore inevitably in key areas of the business. An activity may be delivering customer value, but in such an environment it is likely to have to bear its share of cuts along with everything else. It is also not uncommon for an organisation to shed its good people in an act of unfocused redundancy.

It is possible that there will be a crude attempt to focus cuts by concentrating on the support departments and expecting fewer cuts from front-line customer-supporting departments. Such an approach may be a slight improvement. However, it is likely to leave untouched the waste and profligacy in a 'line' department. Meanwhile, in hacking away at support departments, cuts are made in services that are important for the organisation's success. An example could be cutting recruitment of young people and training, or sidelining the employee-development process to save money. Such aspects may not count for much in terms of 'added value' to customers but they crucially add value to the organisation's assets and should be recognised as such.

Focusing on processes, not on outcomes

In order to focus on what really matters it is essential to be aware of the problems that underlie the issues highlighted by the statistics. A group of managers looking at the analysis in Table 23 could conclude that manpower must be reduced by all except company C. There are, of course, difficult and complex pressures at work here. If the organisation is in difficulties it may not be able to find an alternative quick-fix solution to its problems. Downsizing to put the books in balance may be seen as the only short-term alternative. Even if that is the case it is necessary, having done that, to focus on the strategic issues to prevent a recurrence of the problem in the future. Unless the underlying problems are reviewed and resolved they will re-emerge as problems at some point. It has to be recognised that the employment issue can rarely be resolved by downsizing. In Table 23 it is possible to conclude that numbers of employees are not too high. The issue that has to be investigated is what differences exist in the other companies that lead them to achieve lower numbers of HR staff. Unless that point is recognised and dealt with the problems will remain.

It is therefore very important to look at process. This is particularly important in Table 23 for companies B, D, and F. A failure to do so will usually lead to the indiscriminate cuts that slowly debilitate many organisations. Those that prosper will be those that recognise the importance of process. The other issue is whether the benchmark ratio should be set at 23 company employees to each HR employee. The impact of such a benchmark would be serious for all the other companies in the group. For example, company A would have to achieve 160 HR employees to meet that benchmark – which is a reduction of some 70 employees from its current strength. First you must challenge the benchmark by looking at process. If the benchmark holds good and company C is better then the other companies must restructure their processes radically to meet the reduced level. No matter how often employees are exhorted to 'reduce costs', or 'train more', or 'reduce recruitment costs',

Table 23

MANPOWER BENCHMARKS IN ORGANISATIONS

	HR staff in each company						
	Ratio	Org. Employees	Productivity	Training	Resourcing	Other	Total HR
	1	2	3	4	5	6	7
Company A	(16)	3684	42	38	64	86	230
Company B	(14)	4387	57	63	82	122	324
Company C	(23)	6210	38	52	73	115	278
Company D	(14)	5304	72	68	103	142	385
Company E	(15)	2986	17	25	64	89	195
Company F	(13)	3007	33	35	95	74	237

Notes

Column 1 is a ratio of organisation employees to each HR employee; a high number is therefore 'better' than a low number (eg Company C is apparently better than the others, while F is the worst).

unless the processes and culture are studied as issues the reductions will not be achieved. Rather, employees will scurry around spending time and effort in ensuring that a culprit is found who is not themselves. Success, therefore, is a matter of analysing the few key issues; of keeping what matters in perspective and dealing with the processes. The outcome is very important; in some circumstances it can be all that matters. If you are seeking to achieve more with less, the exhortation to 'cut costs' will lead nowhere unless the underlying process – what people actually do – is also scrutinised.

None of this is new. In the 1970s and 1980s managers were exhorted to 'keep it simple stupid' or to 'stick to the knitting' (Peters and Waterman 1982). What is new is that benchmarking has provided a common perspective in which various initiatives come together. This 'benchmarking' is likely to be different from all the other change initiatives that managers have been through, such as MBO (Management by Objectives), OD (Organisation Development), TQ or TQM (Total Quality

Management), or B5-5750/ISO-9000 and IIP (Investors in People). All of these changes, in varying ways, stressed the customer and the importance of adding value, but benchmarking has locked in the notion of comparison and process as a way forward to make step changes in the organisation. This focus on customers is important, for one solution is to establish standards of service required by internal users and to meet those standards. Benchmarking can assist in identifying the best practice among processes that exist.

Analysing the process: standards of service

How can HR meet this need in practice? The example given in Table 24 shows the criteria used to assess the success of the development and appraisal process in one organisation. Such an analysis of the standards of service of what an appraisal and development process is expected to deliver would be new for many organisations. In the standard approach there is paper, form-filling and a general tendency towards policing. The example shows an organisation that found better practices after benchmarking. It decided that bureaucracy could be discarded in favour of simplicity, with responsibility for development and appraisals being passed to participants. A reduction in form-filling with brisk and to-the-point discussions. The board envisaged limited intervention, which consisted of setting simple but clear objectives. The point is that when the criteria are set down the organisation has something to compare with other organisations to see whether they do things better. Benchmarks can then be established. If the process, or part of it, cannot be justified against the criteria then part of it must be changed or perhaps the criteria must be changed.

The recruitment process is another area of HR that is frequently the subject of criticism by management colleagues. A survey undertaken in one company found what is probably a familiar litany of complaints about the recruitment process. The points made are summarised in Table 25. Again, in benchmarking recruitment performance you must have criteria against which you can measure performance. You can then debate the performance with other managers. Before you can

Table 24

MEASURING THE DEVELOPMENT AND APPRAISAL SCHEME: AGREED CRITERIA

1	The purpose is to measure and reward performance and determine development needs separately.
2	It shall consist of brisk and to-the-point discussions taking place regularly, with an annual review.
3	There shall be a minimum of documentation and form-filling (a target maximum of two single A4 sheets).
4	The responsibility for the success of the appraisal and development shall rest with the parties involved.
5	The board requires that:

- business objectives be set each year and reviewed
- assessments of performance be completed each year
- assessments of potential be completed every two to three years
- the staff involved recognise that development is taking place
- the procedure apply to all employees.

From the HR Group

Table 25

COMPLAINTS ABOUT THE RECRUITMENT PROCESS

1	Takes too long.
2	Manager does not know what is happening, and does not understand how grades are determined.
3	Advertisements are poorly placed in press.
4	Advertisements are turgid and unattractive.
5	Job titles kill any enthusiasm of likely candidates.
6	Insufficient responsibility of the manager in appointing.
7	Takes too long to get an appointee to start after a person leaves.

From *Industrial Relations Review* 1990 (quoted in Bramham 1994)

conclude the discussion satisfactorily it is important that the process be clearly set out. An example of a recruitment process is given in Table 26. Although from a large organisation, this procedure is not exceptional. The procedure has various opportunities for delay. There are many pass-overs (eg from head count to job evaluation, and then to employee relations for union comment) and a number of authorisation steps (eg director's signature required, and authority for advertising and

Table 26

RECRUITMENT PROCESS

☐ Employee leaves.

☐ Job requisition raised.

☐ HR assesses against budget in head count section.

☐ HR assesses grade in job evaluation.

☐ HR assesses task in union terms.

☐ Requisition returned for signature by director.

☐ Requisition returned to recruitment.

☐ Job advert placed (internal/external).

☐ If external, seek approval of trade unions and director.

☐ Applicants write in for form.

☐ HR acknowledges and sends form.

☐ HR pre-sorts application.

☐ HR sends short-list suggestion to manager.

☐ Manager agrees shortlist.

☐ HR and manager agree interview date.

☐ HR invites applicants.

☐ HR and manager interview applicants.

☐ Recommended applicant to superior.

☐ Letter of offer to candidate subject to references.

☐ Candidate's references checked and medical.

☐ Candidate receives formal offer.

☐ Candidate starts after notice period.

From the HR Group

the actual appointment are needed). With such a complex procedure the opportunity for mistakes, and therefore referrals, will occur. These hand-offs avoid a person having to make a decision, allowing the recipient the opportunity to refer it back for correction. The point is that in order to benchmark

Table 27

BENCHMARKING HR

	A	B	C	D
HR employees as % of organisation	4.7	2.9	1.6	2.1
Recruitment – days to fill post*	152	61	33	47
Trainers as % of organisation	1.1	0.5	0.2	0.2
Days training per trainee	1.3	3.4	4.0	3.6
Days training per employee	8	11	13	9
Absence/days lost per annum	7.5	9.2	6.7	6.9
Labour turnover %	6	6.7	4.5	5.1
Industrial action days lost	0.7	–	0.9	–

*Excludes advertising time and notice period.

Taken from the HR Group

anything you have to know the detail of what you are expected to change.

You could undertake a benchmarking exercise at the first level of the type shown in Table 27. This type of first-level operationally directed benchmarking, discussed in Chapter 2, is important and legitimate but it is not the whole story. From your experience, and looking at Table 27, it is possible to conclude that not all is well in your HR department A. The numbers of employees are higher than in the other companies and trainers are also high in number. On the other hand, the number of days training delivered appears to be low. Absence, labour turnover (as long as you have accounted for short-service leavers, which tend to increase the overall rate) and industrial action are all examples of factors which can tell you something about the general health of an organisation – the so-called withdrawal from work pattern (Bramham 1988). A problem in the organisation is revealed in the first column. Even if you set generous benchmarks and do not try to meet the best, the performance gap is still going to mean significant change. In this case Tables 26 and 27 refer to the same organisation. Clearly, the long and tedious recruitment process has a bearing on the length of time taken to recruit a new employee.

Table 28

ANALYSING HR PROCESSES

I First Level
Routine operational non-core processes – canteen, cleaning, administration of recruit-ment, some training.

2 Second or Business Level
Operational core processes – selection decisions to an agreed policy, absence control, training of key business categories.

3 Third or Strategic Level
Strategic processes – setting standards for all key HR processes, overall control of pay strategies and trade union negotiations.

Scrutinising non-core processes

What must be done with non-core processes – among which will be included most HR processes? They must be rigorously scrutinised to ensure the best possible service at a reasonable price. An example of the categorisation of the various approaches is given in Table 28. In this example matters such as cleaning could be outsourced if they can be done better and cheaper by other organisations. On the other hand, while recruitment administration can be handled in that way the selection decision which is still operational is kept in-house because of its long-term impact. All HR processes should be thoroughly benchmarked and all processes that remain after streamlining should be market tested. Can they be purchased cheaper outside? Is someone better able to provide this service? Is the organisation spending too much time and energy on this matter? What does an HR benchmarking exercise look like when directed at a non-core activity?

After undertaking a benchmarking exercise within the training department of a group of related organisations the position as shown in Table 29 was identified. What this figure shows, particularly for organisation A is the small proportion of training time spent in front of a class or actually doing or supporting training. The first realisation was that trainers attended courses with a trainer colleague, which effectively halves the

Table 29

BENCHMARKING IN A TRAINING DEPARTMENT

I Before benchmarking
Number of half-day sessions per week per employee

	Training organisation			
	A	B	C	D
Single class contact time	–	4	3	6
Joint class contact time (two people)	I	1.5	2	1.5
Preparation time	6	I	2	I
Other time	2	2	I	–

2 After benchmarking
Number of half-day sessions per week per employee

	Training organisation	
	A	Benchmark
Single class contact time	7	4/5
Joint class contact time (ie people)	–	1.5
Preparation time	I	2
Other time	2	I

Notes
Before benchmarking most time was spent on preparation and double-heading on courses. After the changes, the benchmark was beaten and productivity increased. In conjunction with other changes productivity improved by over 300 per cent.

trainer's productivity as shown under 'joint class contact time'. As you can see, two people attending a one-day session is, in terms of productivity, only a half-day of training for each. After a review, trainers were allocated one to a course and any support needed was made available during the sessions. That move led to phenomenal improvements in productivity.

By other approaches (such as developing a shared bank of material rather than having each trainer develop their own) each trainer's contact time with students rose to an average of 64 per cent in organisation A – an increase of some 300 per cent! In this case the benchmark was bettered and a very much livelier and happier training department resulted. Of course, this was not appropriate for all training. Some types of training requires two or more trainers and the system had to be sufficiently flexible to accommodate that. In the final outcome there were so few cases where double-heading was essential that they could not be recorded in these average statistics. Another result was the stimulus that was provided among organisations B, C, and D to look at some of their own practices. As a result the benchmarking exercise had a beneficial effect on all the participants.

It is important again to recognise that it was essential to look at processes to achieve this change. Simply telling trainers to improve productivity would have had a limited effect. In this case the shared data bank of course material and not doubling up trainers were two simple ideas that led to significant savings. The same sort of approach must be applied to all non-core processes which will result in:

☐ some processes being changed radically
☐ some processes being outsourced
☐ some processes being stopped altogether
☐ some activities being transferred to core processes.

The first two of these have been discussed above and we should now look at the last two.

Stopping and combining processes

After a benchmarking exercise it is not unusual to discover the type of analysis shown in Table 30, where for each procedure in the HR department the results of surveying users are identified. It is then a short step to proposing a solution. These examples are given only to illustrate the possibilities. It is missing an opportunity provided by benchmarking if this is not done for all of the key HR processes. Inevitably there will be problems, but the problem is not usually finding a solution but in delivering its implementation against those who oppose the change. There will be trade union suspicions and line managers will make mistakes. All such changes must be carefully introduced after full training. It is true that some activities will have to be stopped altogether. There is something about any business activity that results in the accumulation of dead wood over a period of time. Activities that at one time seemed essential are continued as a matter of unquestioned routine. Some non-core processes should be combined into core processes and handed to the value-adding process manager. Functions (and this applies equally to finance, marketing, corporate planning and the rest) have a tendency to develop ideas that go far beyond key business drivers. It should be apparent that any routine administrative roles being exercised by HR will be rigorously scrutinised as part of a benchmarking exercise. Comparisons with other organisations will quickly identify where extra resources are used which increase costs, or where a procedure has the appearance of embellishment for its own sake and should be removed. This approach to HR benchmarking will increase the influence of HR. This is because HR people have the ability to turn the organisation's search for competitive advantage through benchmarking into an organisation change programme with people at the centre.

The way of dealing with these issues is to have an HR unit that acts both as an executive arm and internal consultancy. It implies an HR unit that establishes with the 'board' the strategic benchmarking standards in terms of equal opportunities, recruitment and advertising, manpower levels, remuneration, employee development, canteens and car schemes and so on. Some ideas are further developed in Chapter 10. In this role of standard setting and business improvement HR expertise can operate at the top table where strategic decisions are made. It is particularly important for the human dimension of many strategic change decisions to be taken into account before the decision is made. It is important to note that a frequent cause of the failure of benchmarking (and much criticism of business process re-engineering) is the failure to take people along with the change. The people issues are, as ever, crucial (Willmot 1994; Mumford and Hendricks 1996) and without their support changes cannot be made.

To change or not to change?

What happens when a benchmarking exercise has been undertaken and it shows that another organisation or other

Table 30

BENCHMARKING PROCESSES AND POSSIBLE SOLUTIONS

Process	Results	Solution
Recruitment	Costly	— streamline procedure cut-out steps, hand-offs and pass-overs.
	Over-involvement of professional staff	— give selection decisions to line process owners.
	Longer time than competitors to hire	— HR to set standards and agree them with line managers.
Development	Exclusive	— apply to all employees.
	Time-consuming	— streamline and reduce paperwork to best practice.
	Lack of ownership	— pass responsibility to line; HR-set standards to be met.
Reward	Secretive/no one knows	— introduce line evaluators and brief-out schemes.
	Bureaucratic	— reduce paperwork and shorten job descriptions.
	Lack of ownership	— line evaluators.
	Board fear of loss of cost control	— evaluators to meet board cost targets, and HR to set criteria.
Industrial relations	Secretive	— second line managers to act as negotiators.
	Lengthy meetings	— set agreed times for meetings.
Discipline/ absence and grievances	Costly and time-consuming	— reduce and streamline.
	Over-involvement of HR managers opting out of decisions	— only at final stages. — full responsibility to line for decisions. — line working to standards set by HR.

organisations generally achieve better results, over a much quicker time-scale and with fewer people? What does a bench-marked and changed core-process look like? Perhaps, for example, the benchmarking analysis has shown significant differences in absenteeism, labour turnover, delivery times and manpower levels: the sort of result that might be found is given in Table 31. In this example, from a north-eastern engineering company's benchmarking exercise, it took place with market-ing, finance, training and employee relations to meet the competition by streamlining the servicing and bill payment methods. The benchmarking showed the problem – there were too many pass-overs and hand-offs in the existing procedure, as shown in Table 31. With training and trade union agreement a pilot was established to work in some locations in accordance with the new process in Table 32. Of course, it is essential that the implications of the analysis are interpreted correctly. One process-led employee was in charge of making an appointment, ordering and identifying any parts required, and receiving and clearing the customer's payment. Indeed, this was later extended to include routine selection, development and train-ing decisions which therefore had to be discussed with the process leader/manager. This is shown in the last two points in Table 32.

After that analysis has taken place you may well come to the conclusion that other people are doing much better than you, and that you have to change. In this example it took many years before what were significant changes became accepted, and only in 1994 was the development and necessary infor-mation technology support complete and in place. Taken together with the trade union and employee resistance, and the training changes, one small area such as this took a long time to introduce fully.

Changing existing processes

It is reasonable to look at how a task is done to see whether efficiency savings or quality improvements can be achieved. It is possible to look at the detail of the job to test out this pos-sibility. In HR terms you might seek to improve the number of interviews held by HR staff. Perhaps the selection interviews

Table 31

HR INVOLVEMENT IN BUSINESS BENCHMARKING

Existing process
☐ Customer calls and appointment made.
☐ Fitter contacted and calls.
☐ Determines fault.
☐ Orders part.
☐ Part sent by stores to depot.
☐ Depot informs customer contact section.
☐ Customer contacted to arrange visit.
☐ Fitter calls and installs part.
☐ Fitter passes paperwork to billing.
☐ Bill sent to customer.
☐ Customer pays bill.

Table 32

HR INVOLVEMENT IN BUSINESS PROCESS

Revised process
☐ Customer calls and appointment made.
☐ Fitter calls, determines fault:
– checks part availability through mobile computer
– arranges second visit.
☐ Part sent to fitter's home.
☐ Fitter calls to install part:
– hands over bill and receives payment
– clears credit card through mobile computer.
☐ Fitter discusses future recruitment needs with process manager.
☐ Development and training needs assessed within the process.

themselves can be shortened, or the administrative routines speeded up. Many organisations ask candidates to pre-complete acknowledgement cards, thus reducing the typing load in the organisation.

Other organisations have successfully redesigned application forms to ease the interviewing process. Many others have successfully learnt to write advertisements so that they are much more specific. Many advertisements may have been written in too general a manner allowing hundreds of candidates to think they are right for the job, although it is important not to make illegal discriminatory statements – all of the requirements must be necessary to meet the needs of the job. Simply using arbitrary criteria to exclude potential applicants is unacceptable, and could be illegal.

Many organisations will already have been through rounds of cuts and improving productivity that will have squeezed out costs within the existing processes. When your organisation reaches the position where people are working long hours unwillingly, over long periods, or when they no longer enjoy their job, you must consider whether more cost savings of existing processes are possible – or even a good idea. Clearly, you should try to remove tasks where you can. A task or process that is removed does not need time and energy spent on redesigning it!

Elapsed time *v* process time

Why is it that when you order something through the post you are faced at the end with the dread words 'Please allow 28 days for delivery'? You know that your order has to be opened, and the cheque or credit card approved. Then it is necessary to place the item in a bag and post it. True, larger items will need wrapping, which will take a few minutes, but why 28 days? The process time in this case is probably around 10 minutes. This is the time actually spent on implementing the order. Where do the other 27 days 23 hours and 50 minutes go? Even allowing for weekends and eight-hour days, the lost time is still 159 hours and 50 minutes!

So where is the missing time? Elapsed time and process time can be brought much closer together. When you undertake an initial process with a mail-order catalogue you find that your order is fulfilled the next day. You also know that the answer lies there – if there is no motivation to sort out internal processes within an organisation then the cycle time for the process cannot be reduced. In recruitment for example, when an employee leaves this can automatically trigger an advertisement. The time allowed for applications cannot be dramatically shortened but the process can be simplified by setting the date for interviews at the outset. This avoids the need to try to scramble diary dates nearer the interview, which inevitably wastes time and money. You could even move to 'exception medicals' requiring candidates to fill in a confidential medical questionnaire. The successful candidate would be interviewed by a doctor only if the questionnaire highlighted a particular problem. Perhaps a nurse could be available to pre-assess likely candidates in much the same way. It is possible to bring elapsed time much closer to process time by such approaches. The important point is to recognise the concept. It is about serving the customer because the catalogue company has shown it can be done. Benchmarking results will embarrass your organisation by the speed with which some processes are completed by other organisations.

Reducing pass-overs, hand-ons, hand-offs and authorisation steps

When trying to prepare an outline plan in benchmarking it is essential to reduce the number of steps to an absolute minimum. Each time the documentation in a process has to go to another section or department for some other action then the elapsed time increases. In the example in Table 27 there are many pass-overs and hand-ons that require scrutiny and, in some cases, authorisation. These include sending the requisition to

☐ HR
☐ head count control
☐ job evaluation
☐ industrial relations.

Each one will probably result in a delay of a day or so. Why cannot these 'pass-overs' be reduced? The best practice organisation that you come across in benchmarking will certainly have investigated and found solutions to those problems.

Authorisation steps are different from pass-overs, although the effect may be similar. In the example in Table 26 there are a number of authorisation steps. These include:

☐ HR checks the personnel requisition
☐ requisition signed by director
☐ if external advertisement, seek TU approval, seek Director's approval
☐ short-list sent to manager
☐ applicant recommended to superior
☐ medical authority for appointment sought.

Perhaps the number of authorisation steps can be reduced. There is certainly some logic behind these steps, which are drawn from a north-eastern engineering company. For example, the organisation was going through a significant change and was threatening redundancies. In going along with the change the unions needed some reassurance that new people would not be brought in unnecessarily. One service organisation in Leeds saw itself as being in a serious position and required all jobs to go to the MD before they were filled. In the case mentioned above there is a problem of such authorisation steps. When the MD demanded an explanation of why manpower had increased the HR department was able to produce a list showing that the new jobs had all been authorised by the MD! That throws up another problem of having more authorisation steps. Apart from increasing cycle time when something is passed up for authorisation, it also relieves more junior people from having to take the decisions they should properly be taking. The strategic view would be to establish budgets, targets and standards and then make the managers accountable for their delivery.

Processes *v* functionalism

There is, however, a bigger problem in reducing hand-offs and authorisation steps that is at the heart of a process-led organisation. A temptation is to try to change processes within their existing organisational framework. If the intention is to reduce costs significantly, or to have a dramatic increase in quality, this will certainly fail and is one of the reasons benchmarking fails, as will be discussed in Chapter 13. It is necessary to tackle the fundamental issue of how the processes are organised across departments and not just within them.

There are a series of points that must be looked at. The traditional organisation is built on functional lines. In such a structure, tasks are split up into various component parts and undertaken by knowledge professionals. This is the classic division of labour. It worked well while the purpose was to streamline production into a series of identical tasks and products. The approach worked well until customers became more demanding and employees became better educated.

The idea that tasks could be grouped on other than knowledge divisions was not something that most managers could have contemplated. The tasks required specialised knowledge and the only efficient way of coping with that requirement was to divide up the job so that each part was undertaken by a different person. Gradually this approach grew into functions that left the line managers languishing somewhere down the hierarchy desperately trying to make the organisation work – although perhaps secretly happy that the manager, not being in charge, could not be blamed if things went wrong. In fact, that was a result of functionalisation that had probably not been expected – no one was in charge and no one, except perhaps the MD or CEO, was responsible.

Changes threatening functional power

The demanding customer

There have now been three changes affecting the functional structured organisation. First, and most importantly, the demands of the customer for better service have meant that a functionally divided process is no longer appropriate. It is simply not possible with all the hand-offs and authorisation steps inherent in functional processes also to have a slick procedure with low cycle times. Customers would ask questions and require adaptations to products or services, and if the person dealing with the customer could not handle the queries the customer would go elsewhere.

The educated workforce

The second change has been a better educated and more literate workforce. As processes become better understood, employees could be given greater responsibility over tasks and processes. There is nothing new in this aspect, of course. Both for reasons of improving customer service and providing more fulfilling jobs, car manufacturers, for example, established production lines based on teams in the 1960s. Each change was an assault on traditional functions that has since gathered pace.

Information technology solutions

The third crucial development that was required was the ability to have experts who could readily answer complicated questions. Significant advances could be made if these experts could be available at the touch of a button. One example of this is the change already described in Table 31. The problem of ordering a part, supplying, fixing and billing was a very complicated process. It became four activities grouped into one function as shown in Table 32. Here you can see the crucial importance of IT solutions in managing operations. It is no longer necessary to check with a store person, because the computer checks the inventory directly. It is no longer necessary to pass documentation to scheduling, because the computer records the employee's movements (and will then reallocate work if the employee is ill or unavailable).

At present it is possible to consider that expert systems of this nature have only just begun to edge out many roles from the enterprise. A great many decisions taken by experts require apparently complex yes/no type answers, but they are complex because of the myriad rules that surround them. Where judgement is not involved these activities are now handled routinely by computers in simple repetitive but very complex tasks such as payroll and pension calculations. Those with long memories will recall the large numbers of payroll clerks employed in organisations where now there are two or three people. It is the same with more complex tasks such as accounting, law, pensions, management and health. The IT impact will be devastating on jobs in those predominantly management and middle-class professions. The significance of this is remarkable.

This is benchmarking with a vengeance. It is now possible to contemplate the grouping of previously functional tasks into a truly process-led organisation. In such a scenario key organisational processes are identified and all the operational support processes are detached from functions and passed to be part of that process. In the example in Table 31 all activities such as selection decisions, absence control, trade union discussions, routine training, and so on are passed to form part of the new process in Table 32. One word of caution here is that the process organisation is not a functional system run by a line manager. A truly process-centred organisation means the line process owner or manager actually making selection decisions and dealing with trade unions, and so on. Simply passing HR staff to the manager may be appropriate in the short term but it is not process management, and the activities are still split off from the process they are concerned with.

Summary and conclusion

This chapter has looked at the issue of process as part of benchmarking. It has stressed that while much can be done with first-level analysis of ratios and metrics there is generally a limit to their usefulness. When you need to look still further you will inevitably have to concern yourself with matters of process. This requires an analysis of processes into core and non-core activities. Some can be removed and some combined. The really big benchmarking gains will come from a comparison with other organisations that will show up delays in your own processes. These will be costly and manpower-intensive and will be in the areas of elapsed time versus process time, reducing the numbers of pass-overs (or hand-ons) and the opportunities for delay in hand-offs and authorisation steps, and the better use of expert IT systems to remove wasteful differentiation of jobs. The issue of process has important implications for functions and it is therefore essential to look at the best way that an HR function can add value – this is the subject of the next chapter.

6

ADDING VALUE TO THE ORGANISATION

Line departments and support services

One purpose behind benchmarking is to scrutinise overhead support services and cut out as much of the dead wood and non-revenue generating activities as possible. It has been said repeatedly (Hammer Conference 1995) that a support service does not 'add value'. That is, support services do not add anything to the product sold that the customer is willing to pay for. This chapter will look at adding value and will consider whether these writers are correct and what the implications are for HR.

The suggestion is that if you are an internal supplier of a service you cannot 'add value' in the sense in which the term is used. However good a recruitment service you give to the production department, value is not being added – the customer will not pay extra for a good recruitment process! In most organisations support services, along with HR, do not and cannot 'add value' to the product. Support services can only be overheads.

The implications of this for HR are immense. If HR cannot justify its costs, and therefore its existence, in terms of adding value it will justifiably be subject to scrutiny over its continued existence. This is an important point to make, even if it is made with a lack of sensitivity! (Bramham, 1996.) Service providers must not run ahead of wealth production. The rest of this chapter will discuss the idea that HR generally does not add value to the product or service in any direct way. We shall then consider what HR does add. The answer is asset value –

but along with that recognition comes a reality that HR cannot expect to receive more resources that are insufficient even to give to front line operations. HR has constantly to demonstrate that it is aware of this problem and can explicitly justify its demands.

Wealth generation must exist and be able to finance the provision of a service. Furthermore, the service providers should not be in such a pre-eminent position that even with well-meaning intent they determine the end product. The people who are responsible for the product, usually in sales or production, must have the final say. In business this is not such a problem. An organisation will quickly find whether the end result meets the needs of the market-place. Service providers and producers do not determine the product; the customer does. Customers will either buy the product or they will not. The situation is not as clear cut or immediate as that for non-traded service providers, such as much of health or education. It is always easy to justify greater provision of resources for those services. The point is that they are producers, not customers. Leaving producers in the role of customers and asking them what is needed is like leaving rabbits to guard the lettuce. The question as always has to be – who pays? The customer (when there is one) decides but in other circumstances someone must stand in for the customer.

A department such as HR, or an organisation that is not generating income directly for itself, is always in a weaker position to justify any growth in resources that will incur cost. Conversely, a department or organisation that is generating revenue is always going to be in a stronger position to argue that it should have a greater share of resources. It can, with some justice, plead that if the wealth providers are cut or hampered in any way the effect will eventually be a decline in income that will, in turn, require tough action to correct the imbalance.

Selling the support service

It seems sensible, therefore, that support departments in general – and HR departments in particular – should accept that they do not 'add value' in the sense in which the term is generally understood. The customer does not pay more for the product because HR is doing 'it'; therefore 'it' does not add value.

That is not the whole story, of course. There are some 'service' elements that, while they do not directly change the specification of a product, give the customer some less tangible security that they will willingly pay for. There are some interesting developments taking place in the market-place in this direction. The concept of ethical banking is finding favour with customers who are willing to pay (through a risk of smaller dividends, say) for a set of values they believe in. Oxfam has found in their 'café direct' that customers pay more for the certainty of having products that are not made cheaper through exploitation. In HR terms, gas organisations up to the 1990s found it possible to pay for the costs of expensive apprentice training and development programmes through marketing themselves as the 'professionals'. Customers came to some gas companies because they could trust the standards of safety and service that were provided. The customer, therefore, is attracted in some areas of provision of services by the knowledge that resources are spent on ensuring that employees are competent and reliable. This has always been the case, but as customers have become more demanding so their choices have increasingly to be met. A further example may suffice. Many organisations market themselves through 'soundbite slogans' such as 'We are the best', 'We try harder', 'Our people care', and so on. All of this is a reference, not to the product itself, but to the manner in which the product is delivered. Having problems, or making mistakes, or being out of stock is not the problem. Such difficulties will always occur and this does not drive customers away. The issue is the manner, speed and efficiency with which any problem is resolved, or any out-of-stock item is made available and, of course, how often these circumstances occur.

In terms of adding value it is essential to keep this in perspective. Customer loyalty is a fragile commodity and can quickly evaporate in the face of the cost of a product or service being on the wrong side of a price differential. The result can be a massive loss of business, as many former utilities have found. When this happens overheads will be hacked away. This is to be taken as a warning that support services must not let their costs get out of control, but it also gives some clues about selling the support service.

Statutory and political requirements

It is essential to recognise that while all the administrative non 'value-adding' processes should be closely scrutinised it does not mean that they should all be stopped. There are other factors that affect a decision to retain a service. As well as selling services that can indirectly 'add value' to the product or service sold there are considerations such as statutory, regulatory and code of practice requirements. In HR terms it is essential that managers apply the law correctly on, say, equal opportunities. It cannot be ignored merely because the customer does not want to pay for it. It should also be pointed out that since other organisations have to meet the same requirements, this will mean similar costs being loaded as 'overheads' on all similar organisations. Benchmarking is emerging in a period of trade globalisation. It is perhaps appropriate to note that one country or group of countries cannot let costs get out of line with its competitors any more than a single organisation can. In this global market-place, where communications backed up by information technology make rapid decisions and ordering possible, any trading block has to watch its competitors' costs.

This applies to aspects other than purely statutory matters. Political issues can be equally, and perhaps more, pressing. Although backed up by legislation, it is largely political pressure that is driving equal opportunities forward in many organisations. Indeed, people who have been responsible for dealing with statutory requirements know how easy it is to handle a purely statutory framework. Taking equal opportunities (or rather, sex discrimination) as an example, much of the growth of HR is due more to the politics of the issue than its legislative heritage. At this point it is simply necessary to register that, in any desire to remove overhead costs that do not add value, it is important to reflect that statutory and political costs cannot be ignored. They are a responsibility that must be accounted for.

Exaggerating statutory needs

One note of caution should be sounded here. There is a tendency to exaggerate the requirement to meet statutory needs. One example could be the visual display unit and other health and safety regulations that were introduced in the late 1980s under European directives. Many organisations went too far and established detailed policies and inspection requirements that were brought about by their specialist so-called support service departments and their enthusiastic interpretation of the legislation.

The problem with assessing 'value' and whether something is needed under legislation is in understanding the essence of what is required and then applying it. Managers may see the absurdity of what is being proposed but then they do not apply those parts where action really is necessary. If a manager was neglecting only the excesses, that would be satisfactory. The problem comes because the manager may not be in a position to make that judgement accurately between the essential and 'the nice to have'. The result can be lukewarm implementation of changes. It is not necessary to look further than health and safety issues, equal opportunities codes of practice and visual display regulations to find examples of this. In assessing value, anything that does not add value or asset value must be rigorously scrutinised. It is far better to establish realistic benchmarked targets and work up to them, than to go overboard and finish with nothing.

The HR unit, value and drivers

So what of the activities provided by an HR department? Surely they do valuable work and therefore 'add value'? Generally, and unfortunately, the answer is that they do not! The organisation may have an up-to-date appraisal and development scheme but the customer does not care to pay for it. Therefore it does not add value at the point of the trade. What does an HR department do in terms of adding value? Reflecting on the appraisal and development scheme as an example the correct thing to do is to recognise that value is not being added in the important financial sense. What you are doing is adding value to the asset base. It is therefore necessary to be able to demonstrate this to everyone's satisfaction.

This imposes a whole new set of problems for the HR unit. In this environment it becomes necessary to justify what is being done against set criteria. These criteria have to be argued through with those managers who are in effect paying for the service. The question that has to be asked is, What are the key drivers of the organisation? If a particular process was never done again, who would suffer? If the HR department is confident of its role, benchmarking will not expose it to questions that it cannot answer.

Surveys have shown (Bramham 1997) that much of the activity that is carried out by HR departments is routine administration and not a key driver of the organisation. While selection is essential, it could be done just as well, and probably better and cheaper, by the line manager – particularly if HR can set and monitor the standards that are used by line managers. This points to the way ahead for HR. This brings the discussion to a point where HR has to ask itself, What is its role in the organisation? The suggestion being made here is that in most cases HR does not 'add value' directly to the product or service. The implication of this is that such services as those provided will be seen as overheads and will therefore be subject to continual threat.

The solution is for HR to take the initiative on change and make its justification of HR benchmarking a radical review and restructuring of HR activities. In a time that regards the customer as pre-eminent it is always difficult for personnel to make an operational impact. With the increasing sophistication of organisations and customers alike the solution is to present the HR function as a key contributor to the strategic focus of the organisation. This is the subject of Chapters 9 and 10.

Many organisations no longer even have the destructive industrial relations climate that was important to the status of 'personnel departments' through the 1970s and 1980s in the UK. Benchmarking will force these issues to be investigated, if a financial crisis has not got there first. The time is ripe to undertake a benchmarking exercise and arrange an orderly transfer of process-supporting routines to be managed as part of a core process by process owners.

Asset value

HR must see itself as adding asset value in a strategic context. The question that has to be asked is, How much does HR add to the assets that the organisation has? Every time training takes place assets are added. People become capable of carrying out more skills and therefore of helping to create better products and services. This is the idea that lay behind 'human asset accounting' or 'human resource accounting' in the 1970s and 1980s. This was an attempt to ascertain the value of people to the organisational balance sheet, by giving them a value. It was not a success in itself, but it focused attention on the absurd notion that people are to be regarded as a cost. On the contrary, human activity is perhaps arguably the only true asset that exists. Even the oil or gas in the ground has to be extracted by employees! Some would argue that willing miners are easier to find than oilfields but that ignores the ability of employees to affect the business and the wages paid in oilfields! It is necessary to pay wages but you also have to buy capital assets or fees to extract minerals from the ground. The modern equivalent of human asset accounting is human value management (Fitz-Enz 1990). This assumes that people are assets and the purpose of developing and training them is to add value to those assets.

The value-creating process is given schematically in Figure 8. If the HR department cannot 'add value' it can add to the assets in terms of the people employed. The model recognises that the enabling processes of style and managing people affect the asset-creating processes of training, development, performance management, and so on. These, in turn, affect people and they will have social consequences – all part of building a healthy organisation. This feeds through into business results, and whether value has been added is determined by the customer. Many organisations will find this comforting, but it comes with a responsibility that must be fulfilled. In a modern competitively driven organisation there will always be a struggle over the allocation of available resources. It is therefore important that HR departments and line managers with people management responsibilities set out specifically what they expect from a particular programme and what the asset-creating

Figure 8
ADDING ASSET VALUE

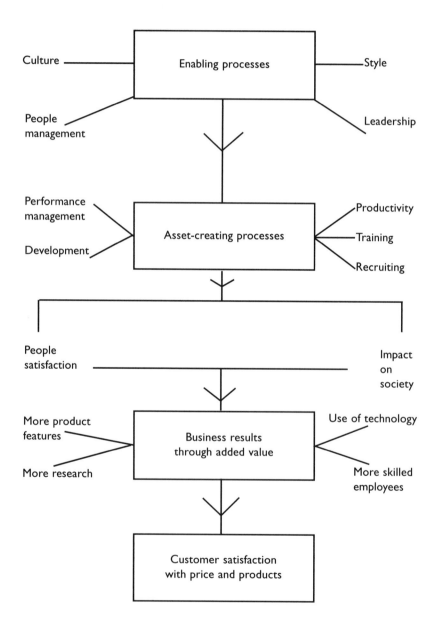

impact it is believed will result. This is the way that resources will be allocated to HR activity.

In people terms, not much activity is given to detailed financial accounting. This, however, is no reason why the rigorous control of costs should not be undertaken. Indeed, it should – and with more rigour and questioning than would apply to non-overhead activities. The suggestion is often made that human resource benefits such as these cannot be measured in financial terms. We can perhaps learn something from the Japanese idea of *kaizen* – meaning gradual unending improvement. This is the idea that the process should be the focus of attention. Improvements are made by gradually improving the way things are undertaken. These process changes can be analysed and assessed in a number of ways:

☐ Does it improve quality?

☐ Does it add to assets?

☐ Will that lead to measurable quality improvements?

☐ Does it reduce costs?

☐ Does it reduce cycle time?

Table 33 suggests some ways in which HR work can be allocated. This transfer takes place after a benchmarking exercise to determine the most effective way of handling the changes. There will be an initial cost because managers must be trained to run these activities, or manage the personnel officers who are transferred to undertake them. Personnel staff also will benefit from more intense exposure to line department activities and their career prospects will be enhanced. In 1990, after a benchmarking management review of HR performance, a north-eastern engineering company began transferring training jobs to line managers on rotation. The employees in those roles quickly became recognised as among the best trainers.

If benchmarking leads to this sort of change, HR will set the detailed HR standards of behaviour and approaches that the line must adhere to. In this scenario HR adds asset value by policy formulation, standard-setting and monitoring the organisation's achievement of its HR aims. In the strategic column in Table 33 can be seen some of the strategic roles that are envisaged as an HR responsibility.

Table 33

TRANSFERRING HR OPERATIONS TO THE LINE

	Operational – to line	*Strategic/other – to HR*
Training	induction courses skills courses on-the-job training	one-off training new issue training
Recruitment	all selection process handling interviews graduate workshops (the 'milk round')	one-off specialist recruits advertising (through an agency)
Rewards and job evaluation	recommending pay increases writing job descriptions agreeing jobs with employees evaluating jobs with other managers	senior executive senior executive roles
Attendance	attendance monitoring warning procedures	potential industrial tribunals

Discipline	all phases of disciplinary
	   procedures
		support at final appeals
		involvement in
		   dismissal

Records	input once through pay direct access to managers	overall control of HR/ IT system

Staffing	managers decide within
	   manpower budget
		retention of manpower
		   budget unless controlled
		   by financial budget

Employee relations	managers handle most
	   situations through
	   subsidiarity
		retention of main
		   negotiations

These tasks include some operational roles that it is not sensible to devolve. This includes one-off provision of such aspects as organisation-wide benchmarking training. Of course, in order for HR to have sufficient resources, line employees would be transferred to HR for the duration of the exercise. HR would also be available to give specialist advice covering the whole field of HR activity.

The basic difference in this scenario is that HR people become strategists and advisers rather than doers. One alternative is to establish the existing HR function as a cost centre – rather like an internal consultancy service (IDS 1997). In this case it is still necessary to have a separate HR department establishing policy and exercising strategic control but it is an entirely reasonable approach, particularly if a genuine free market exists.

As part of the setting of standards and reviewing performance there is no reason why measurable criteria cannot be given for development, training and recruitment and all other HR activities. Every piece of training that takes place should have measurable outcomes. It is difficult, but it can be done and is carried out successfully by many organisations. If carried out rigorously the benchmarking exercise will quickly highlight those training courses that do not add to people's skills, and which should be changed or stopped. Measurable criteria can even be established for unlikely aspects such as culture, employee attitudes and customer satisfaction. Some possible ways are set out in Chapter 3 on organisational mapping. Such techniques can be used to assess the extent to which assets are being enhanced within the organisation.

Summary and conclusion

An HR unit that does not take the lead in this area is bound to feel the frustration of not getting a share of resources and of seeing significant chances for creating asset value being lost. Benchmarking will create the environment in which HR costs are put under the microscope. It is important to recognise that HR is once removed from the value-adding processes. This will always create tensions in situations where costs are under pressure. HR activities add to the organisation's assets, and it is far better to anticipate the pressure and take the initiative in proposing the transfer of many HR operational activities to line managers. HR, as part of this transfer, is in a better position to insist on policies and standards being established as part of this transfer, and this will ensure that the organisation's HR strategies can be met. It will also enhance the HR department's claim to be the guardian of the organisation's human assets through its leading role in strategic HR management. Only if the organisation adopts a strategic view of people can it hope to create the healthy organisation that is essential to corporate success.

7

METRICS IN BENCHMARKING

What are metrics?

This chapter deals with metrics – that is, the numerical part of benchmarking. Clearly, it is essential to be able to measure. In order to be able to measure benchmarks in a business it is usually necessary to count. Put more simply, 'metrics' is a piece of benchmarking jargon for 'numbers' and the related analysis of them.

Before you can benchmark you must have a view about what you wish the exercise to deliver. There are at least four approaches to gathering metrics, as shown in Table 34. It is important, however, that metrics are viewed within the context of the business. Training costs may seem high compared with those being benchmarked with another organisation. However, if the first company is engaged in high technology and the second company in the routine provision of some low NVQ (national vocational qualification) level task then of course their training costs are different. Training costs will always increase with value-adding work. It is therefore dangerous to make direct comparisons with the metrics of another organisation without understanding their context. Unwarranted conclusions may result if you do.

In looking at benchmarking as in other fields, metrics are usually classified as either 'hard' or 'soft'. Hard data would be absence rates or productivity levels achieved. An example of soft data would be employee views of the organisation. It is 'soft' because there is judgement involved in the data. In this case, the employee's views are determined by many factors that are varied and even outside the strict concern of the organisation; for example, how the person feels about his or her own health.

A normal method of making progress would be to start

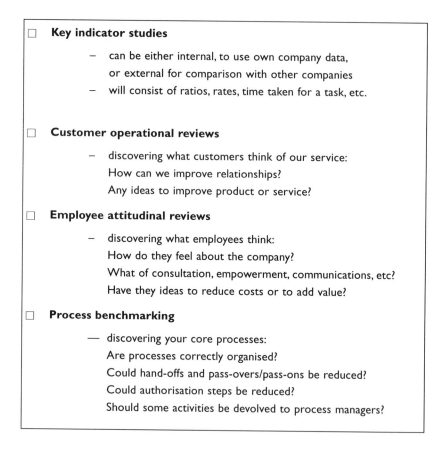

Table 34

GENERIC TYPES OF BENCHMARKING METRICS

☐ **Key indicator studies**

– can be either internal, to use own company data,
or external for comparison with other companies

– will consist of ratios, rates, time taken for a task, etc.

☐ **Customer operational reviews**

– discovering what customers think of our service:
How can we improve relationships?
Any ideas to improve product or service?

☐ **Employee attitudinal reviews**

– discovering what employees think:
How do they feel about the company?
What of consultation, empowerment, communications, etc?
Have they ideas to reduce costs or to add value?

☐ **Process benchmarking**

— discovering your core processes:
Are processes correctly organised?
Could hand-offs and pass-overs/pass-ons be reduced?
Could authorisation steps be reduced?
Should some activities be devolved to process managers?

collecting hard data (costs, absence rates, etc) and then follow that with soft metrics (employee attitudes). It is necessary to make clear that it is not suggested that soft data are somehow inferior. They may be more important to analyse and understand than are hard numerics. Some aspects of process analysis will be concerned with measures of who does what and how long it takes, whereas other measures will include matters of judgement. It is also important to remember what was said about drivers. Is the indicator that is being measured a key factor in your organisation? There is no point being excellent at something if it does not deliver added asset value in some direct and tangible way.

In all cases of benchmarking metrics you can start with a long list of possible measures. You then analyse this list and delete those that are uncollectable or expensive to collect. You must be realistic about the state of your own company's data. Do not be disrespectful to partners by providing data you know are not correct. It is also necessary to keep the metrics under review. Some aspects that are key one year can fade in importance in the next. Look back at how important labour turnover once was to personnel departments. There was a time when it became such an issue that whole businesses grew from it; now it is hardly spoken of. But these metrics and drivers ebb and flow and labour turnover could once again be a defining issue.

Key indicators

Key indicator studies refer to those factors that affect the whole or part of an organisation. The important point is that they are based on factors emanating from the organisation or department and not an analysis of tasks. They are often economic or financial indicators, or rates or time taken.

The decision of which way to go in terms of metrics will depend on what your intention is for benchmarking. If you intend to use benchmarking to assess the general state of your organisation by benchmarking it against other companies and competitors then the adoption of the key indicator approach will work. In this sort of analysis you hope to find a few statistics that are indicative of the state of the organisation. The analysis may be restricted and cover items such as profit, return on investment, employee numbers, absence rates, pay levels and conditions, and so on, which are calculated as ratios or percentages. The problem is that it is impossible to use such analyses to determine a detailed action plan. It is usually necessary to look deeper into both internal and external information in order to ascertain what action is needed, but such analyses are useful for identifying possible problem areas.

Customer and/or employee operational reviews

These are important ways to benchmark the company. Whatever the result of either or both of the key indicator studies, the views of employees and customers will be crucial. Such reviews have some similarities with customer and employee attitude surveys, or even with the industrial relations audits that were common in the 1980s (Bramham 1997). Their purpose is the same – what do our customers and employees think of the service given or of the organisation they work in? An example of the areas to cover in such a survey was given in Chapter 3. With this type of numerical analysis of customers' views it is possible to begin to assess the implications for future profitability or budget provision. For employee reviews the concern is about commitment, loyalty, the way employees are managed, and so on. This is the beginning of an understanding of organisation culture and its effects. The organisation is seeking to peel away the pretence that often exists about people and how they are treated. The intention is to know the extent to which employees support the organisation's aims, their attitude to work, and whether morale is high or low. Only if these aspects are in order can an organisation hope to achieve high performance levels and meet its other objectives. But it should be remembered that these sorts of studies, derived solely from internal comparisons, are of limited value. It is only by benchmarking information against other organisations that your own data begin to have meaning. It is possible to compare results with what other organisations have achieved. In this way the desirable target area for achievement can be benchmarked.

Are the metrics relevant?

One difficulty of metrics in benchmarking is ensuring the validity of the data. It is not uncommon to find that an organisation comes to benchmarking because it feels it has a problem and is looking for techniques to deal with it. This is, of course, healthy because there can be no organisation that does not feel the threat of competitive pressure. However, an organisation may be benchmarking because it is in a significant state of change. The organisation may have gone through some traumatic events such as a take-over or management buy-out, bundling or unbundling, and so on. The first of these two situations is common these days and there will be no prima-facie case to distrust the numbers that the process generates. However, even in these organisations there has to be a healthy questioning of the data. If the strategic-level benchmarking tells you that your organisation is good (or bad) does this accord with the views of managers? Any data refer to the past, and the past may no longer be relevant. This will also throw into doubt the validity of numerical analysis. At the very least such changes will mean that the data will probably put in doubt the value of historical comparisons. Care must be taken in both these situations to ensure that in undertaking numerical analysis the organisation is not following an approach that will mislead rather than illuminate.

It is important to make sure that the metrics that are obtained are relevant and therefore will inform the decisions that are to be made. If, for example, you wish to benchmark performance, unit output and manpower costs you need to reduce the metrics to a simple, easily understood figure. An example of this is given below in the formula:

$$P = O \text{ divided by } C$$

where P = assessed unit of performance

O = unit of output

C = manpower costs

Obviously the comparison will be valid only if the costs and output to which it relates are for comparable types of work. If, for example, you tried to compare sales visits per employee the resulting metrics may be meaningless if the comparators were a company selling brushes and a company selling computer software. The cost structure and sales per employee would be totally different and the resulting numbers meaningless. Even if it is possible to measure and count output, there can still be room for doubt over whether employee costs metrics represent reality. An engineering organisation in the West Midlands undertook a benchmarking study which sought to analyse and compare training costs with outside suppliers. The formula used was effectively as follows:

$$\text{cost one day of training} = \frac{\text{wages paid} + \text{materials} + \text{marketing costs}}{\text{numbers of days of training}}$$

Table 35

BENCHMARKING MARKET TRAINING PRICES

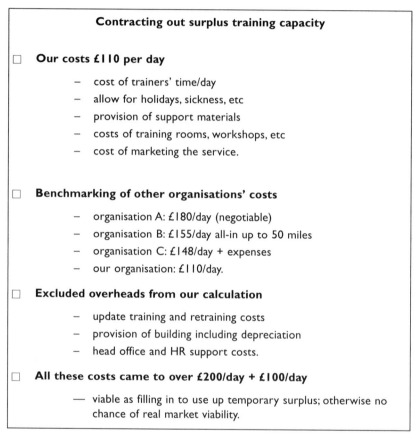

Contracting out surplus training capacity

☐ **Our costs £110 per day**

- cost of trainers' time/day
- allow for holidays, sickness, etc
- provision of support materials
- costs of training rooms, workshops, etc
- cost of marketing the service.

☐ **Benchmarking of other organisations' costs**

- organisation A: £180/day (negotiable)
- organisation B: £155/day all-in up to 50 miles
- organisation C: £148/day + expenses
- our organisation: £110/day.

☐ **Excluded overheads from our calculation**

- update training and retraining costs
- provision of building including depreciation
- head office and HR support costs.

☐ **All these costs came to over £200/day + £100/day**

- viable as filling in to use up temporary surplus; otherwise no chance of real market viability.

The need was to accommodate occasional overcapacity in the training workforce until the organisation needed the trainers again. In this way the trainers became tested in the open market and had to learn to meet other organisational needs. The metrics gave the cost per day of providing trainers and showed that at a certain price extra revenue could also be generated. The organisation decided to sell these services in the marketplace. Benchmarking of market prices shown in Table 35 gave confidence that at least on price the take-up would be sufficient to justify the effort in marketing the training. Not only was the price a good one but the trainers showed themselves capable of holding their own in the market-place and delivering a good service. The business grew until it was decided that extra staff would have to be recruited to fill the need.

It was at this point that difficulties arose. The problem was an inability to keep track of true costs. The reason for this was that selling the spare capacity was not done on the basis of full costs. From the example in Table 35 it can be seen that overhead costs have been ignored. That might have been acceptable while the intention was simply to mop up some spare capacity. There is nothing wrong with such an approach as long as it is clear what is being done, and why. This was not the position in this case. The full costs of providing the service to external customers had been greatly underestimated because overhead costs had not been fully accounted for. As the contracting-out initiative had been intended as a stopgap and all overheads were charged against the core business activity this was not a great problem. It was when the activity became attractive and the department wished to expand it that the failure to include overheads in the original costs became a problem. This mistake is frequently made. It is surprising how easy it is to forget the basis on which original metrics were derived.

Absence metrics

The important point to recognise is that many of the metrics are in areas for which employers will have readily available data. They are particularly useful at the first level of key indicator studies. This is first-level benchmarking, which is used to get a feel for the organisation and its position compared with other organisations. Absence metrics can be used as an example of what information you can get from key indicators that may suggest a problem in a particular area. It may be that the analysis indicates a problem with some specific department. Perhaps the absence rate in your organisation or department is very much higher than it is in similar comparators.

In Table 36 an internal benchmarking exercise highlighted the absence in district D as being out of the ordinary. The analysis in this case showed that district had begun to let

Table 36

AN EXAMPLE OF USING BENCHMARKED METRICS

Absence – days lost per employee			
	1992	1993	1994
District A	6	7	7
District B	7	9	8
District C	8	8	6
District D	13	16	15
Average	9	10	9
Benchmark	6	6	5

Notes:

Districts are all undertaking similar industrial type work.

'Benchmark' is from comparator companies, not an average of these.

absence get out of control. The benchmarking exercise showed that not only had the particular district a high absence level which could not be explained by other factors (eg a much older workforce) but also the trend in that district was of increasing absence levels. This was against a background where absence in the organisation as a whole was improving over the period from 1992 to 1994, although for technical reasons it had risen slightly in 1993. However, the results of an external benchmarking survey was a surprise for all the districts involved. It showed that for the best of them, although their in-company performance was good, even that best compared poorly in external comparisons. This resulted in a lower absence benchmark being set, as shown in Table 36. In this case the benchmark was set below the best of the comparator companies.

That much can be derived from the metrics. However, deciding what action should be taken requires further analysis. This probably has to be in the form of benchmarking the absence processes used to discover whether, for example, other departments carried out more effective absence control procedures or whether the existing procedures were being applied at all. In the particular case of district D in Table 36 process benchmarking revealed that this was indeed the case and that relations in the district had collapsed. The process analysis showed a number of features:

☐ Employees were inadequately, or were not, questioned about absence.
☐ Line managers were avoiding dealing with absence.
☐ Line managers had abdicated their responsibility to HR.
☐ HR felt that managers were inconsistent, lurching from being heavy-handed to opting out.
☐ Trade unions were feared.
☐ There was no attempt to integrate absence control within a total performance process.

The point to register is that first-level indicator benchmarking could indicate that a problem existed in terms of performance, but further analysis was needed to determine the correct course of action to improve that performance.

Customer and employee benchmarking

As an additional analysis it is important to ascertain customer and employee views about how the customer is treated or what the employee thinks about the company. This will entail benchmarking on attitudes and opinions concerning product quality or delivery times, or about whether it is a good place to work, and so on.

This is an area to which some people do not think of applying metrics. The suggestion is that because there is nothing absolute about such matters as product quality or attitudes to work, statistics cannot be collected. There is sufficient evidence to suggest that is not the case. Table 36 was taken from a benchmarking exercise of 1995 where employees' views over a range of issues (not just absence) were sought. Of course, the metrics obtained have to be treated with caution because the areas are judgemental. But it is important to make it clear that it is a lot easier to measure HR areas of work or customer attitudes than many people believe.

Are the metrics available?

When ascertaining which benchmarks to use, one consideration is the availability of your own data and those from other organisations. This is where benchmarking clubs and consultants and similar organisations come into their own. They can provide a ready-made short-cut to access metrics that they have available from their wide range of contacts. It is important to recognise that metrics cannot tell the whole story about an organisation – but neither should they be ignored. For HR people there is a particular problem in trying to persuade people of the worth of their activities. If HR cannot persuade their management colleagues to finance a particular activity then there is a problem that HR has to face. It seems irrational to suggest that the metrics should not be collected because when faced with a difficult decision people make the wrong one! The assumption lying behind such a philosophy is that managers do not understand the true worth of HR and therefore cannot be trusted with hard benchmarking comparisons about it.

For organisations wishing to benchmark HR in some detail, the set of HR measures shown in Appendix 1 at the end of this book may be of particular interest. Although this list may seem extensive, documenting these metrics provides a useful comparison with analyses that you might have in mind for your own organisation. The effort should be to find those indicators that tell you something about the state of HR in the organisation: its health and strength, its ability to withstand changing environments, and the degree to which you have employee support. In 1996 Saratoga (report available to subscribers to Saratoga – see Appendix 2) published the results of their UK benchmarking survey. Organisations in the survey produced data on 60 elements of HR work. These included absenteeism rates and costs, training costs and the ratio of training per employee, reward costs as a percentage of revenue and recruitment costs. The analysis also includes Saratoga's

Table 37

POSSIBLE SOURCES OF METRICS FOR BENCHMARKING

☐	Balance sheets.	☐	Trade journals.
☐	Customers.	☐	Published statistics.
☐	Employees.	☐	Government information services.
☐	Suppliers.	☐	Company publications.
☐	Distributors.	☐	Conferences and presentations.
☐	Newspapers.	☐	IPD library and information.
☐	Professional journals.	☐	IPD branch meetings.
☐	Investment analysis.	☐	Colleges and universities.
☐	Technical libraries.	☐	Trade unions.
☐	*and by personal contact!*		

suggestion of where you should expect to be in the rankings. This idea is important. You may not agree with the suggestions in Appendix 1, but it is essential to understand that it is neither possible nor desirable to be at the top in everything.

The information must, as always, be used sensitively. It is possible for statistics to be wildly wrong for a good reason. For example, an organisation that has decentralised much of its training activity may find it difficult to capture meaningful data to compare with others. However, across the whole range of data, indications of performance and potential problem areas can be obtained.

Other organisations have similar HR databases. The user must look around to see which, if any, of the systems offered has value for the organisation. You should also look in a variety of other places for data, ideas and contacts. Some suggested sources are given in Table 37. It is surprising how much information is available in articles and trade journals. A good source of first-level analytical data is investment analyses and balance sheets. There is a growing use of metrics in management generally. Managers must always look for that extra level of performance. Collecting HR data gives sound information about how people think and behave, and is invaluable to help assess the health of an organisation. Data collection can appear daunting. Time and resources must be invested in it to be successful.

Summary and conclusion

This chapter has highlighted the issue of metrics, or numbers, in benchmarking. It has suggested where they can be obtained and which metrics can be used. The limits of data have also been referred to with a warning not to become obsessed with data collection. For HR people, metrics is not always an area with which they naturally feel at home, often preferring unstructured feelings to 'hard facts'. Often the reality is that much valuable data are 'soft' or even barely susceptible to measurement at all. But the language of business is at bottom £s and $s and not feelings. HR people must be willing to rise to the challenge without at the same time allowing numbers to overwhelm important, but still measurable, qualitative issues.

8

CHOOSING BENCHMARKING PARTNERS

Effective partnering

Benchmarking is concerned with making comparisons with other organisations across a whole range of business activities. In order to compare, you must have something and someone to compare with. How do you go about finding good partners who will work with you? How many should you have? Where will you find them? These are the questions we shall discuss and answer in this chapter.

For a benchmarking partner relationship to be effective there must be some similarity with the organisation being benchmarked against, and an analysis of the type shown in Table 38 should be helpful. Benchmarking assumes a commonality of background conditions. The choice of partners is affected by such factors as availability and size. In a multidivision company it may be possible to find suitable internal comparators carrying out tasks that are sufficiently similar to one's own. Starting at home is, in any case, essential for a clear understanding of processes. You must take time to understand your internal system; how it works and its strengths and weaknesses. You are recommended to map the organisation before you commence external benchmarking. In any event, internal benchmarking is probably necessary in order to have information that is subsequently to be of use to an outside organisation. It is unlikely that an organisation will join in a benchmarking exercise if the process of giving of information is all one way.

The second type of partner that can be chosen is a competitor. The problems here are that, while practices may be

Table 38

SELECTING PARTNERS – WHO IS LIKE YOU?

WHAT DRIVES THEIR PERFORMANCE?

	1	2	3
Internal			
Culture			
Is the organisation	closed		open/empowered?
Size			
No. of employees	<c 250	c 500	1000 +
Capital			
Is the organisation	people-intensive		capital-intensive?
External			
Metrics			
Are they generally	available		not available?
Is the degree of regulatory control	low		highly regulated?
Is the degree of effect of technology	low/stable		continuous change?

From Bramham 1994, adapted from Fitz-Enz

comparable and would therefore provide data of probable direct relevance, there are problems of commercial confidentiality. The closer the information you require is to the core of what they perceive as their competitive advantage, the greater will be the reluctance to share the information. Of course, this is usually less of a problem when benchmarking HR. It is less sensitive and the partner may be willing to proceed with you.

This will not be the case where HR functions have been devolved to process owners. In these circumstances it is often not possible to benchmark the HR part of the process while ignoring the sensitive areas. For example, marketing or production could be very sensitive areas and the competitor, no less than your own company, would wish to keep that knowledge within the company.

Finally, it is possible to refer to industry partners where people are engaged in similar activities but are not in direct competition. These can be either partners within a similar industry who are not competitors, or so-called 'generic' partners who can be anyone else. Here the data will be more generally applicable. Data will also be more easily shared. Of course, against that must be set the difficulty of size. Large companies usually need persuading to compare with a small organisation. If the scale of problems is quite different it is unlikely that any relationship would thrive. A further issue is the geographical distance involved. In most people's experience it helps to have at least some partners close at hand, although with modern technology that is now less of an issue, particularly for data transfer. The possibility of crossing

Table 39

CHOOSING BENCHMARKING PARTNERS

Advantages and disadvantages of types of partner	
Advantages	**Disadvantages**
☐ **Internal**	
People are known to you.	Internal bias.
Good access.	'Not invented here' problems.
Solutions fit and will be	Conceal truth – could be worse
acceptable.	than a competitor.
☐ **Competitive**	
Data directly applicable.	Problem of revealing too much.
Similar market conditions.	Commercial confidentiality.
Comparable practice.	Have they any new ideas?
☐ **Industry/generic**	
Data can be collected and shared.	Size and geographical problems.
Comparable practices.	The organisation may be poorly
Applicable data.	understood.
Fewer sensitive issues.	Faulty comparisons made.

Adapted in Bramham 1994 from Fitz-Enz 1993

cultures is interesting. If you can get past the social barriers that may exist you can pick up many insights into different ways of doing things. The different partners and a summary of their respective advantages and disadvantages are set out in Table 39.

External benchmarking is a two-way street – you must have something to give in return. You must therefore have a good idea of your own organisation's strengths and weaknesses. You have therefore to be clear what you are looking for. What does the company hope to achieve in benchmarking? How many partners are appropriate? Should they differ for each different project. If the organisation is seeking to benchmark one particular area of activity a different partner or partners will be more appropriate than if you wish to benchmark the whole organisation in a massive three- to five-year programme. You should look for four or five partners; any more and you will become bogged down in visits and metrics; any fewer and you are unlikely to have the breadth of practice that will be useful to you.

The stage at which you are in the exercise is a separate and important consideration. Even if you are reasonably committed to full-scale, across-the-board benchmarking in depth, the organisation's needs will be different from what they would be if you were at the exploratory stage. If you are, for example, engaged in a general mapping exercise (see Chapter 3) it may not be necessary to decide on your partners at that early stage.

Where you go looking for partners also depends on the time and resources you have. Clearly, if the organisation is not committing time and resources to the project an external search for partners is likely to be fruitless. It costs time and effort to find the right partner. An organisation will want to know what it can expect in return and is hardly likely to co-operate fully with an organisation that is not able to reciprocate.

Understanding 'Best practice'

It is also necessary to be clear about where the organisation thinks benchmarking is taking it. There is a desire and a need to review and revise practices within the organisation and this is an important consideration in the search for partners. Always assuming that you can identify 'best practice' or 'global standards' (terms used very glibly, it has seemed to some authors), how will you get access to them? Unless your organisation is able to offer some radical benefits in terms of your own 'best practices' (and how is that possible before they have been benchmarked? You simply cannot be sure!), there seems to be no reason why an organisation with best practices will team up with you. You must be realistic. There is a lot of talk about 'best practice' but how do you find it, always assuming you are able to get access to it? It is almost certain that best practice will not be conveniently working away in the factory over the road! You have to ask questions, attend conferences and seminars and in these ways you will find examples of the level of performance you would be proud of. It is essential in the early phases of the project to be realistic about best practice and accept that you use the best available after your initial search. It is also necessary to register that there is something that sounds final about best practice. It can always be bettered, and eventually it will be. Do not be afraid of beating the best if you think you can.

Understanding performance drivers

In choosing a partner or partners it is also important to be aware of what drives performance in your own and your partner's organisation. Performance drivers are the crucial group of factors that determine what makes an organisation tick. They will include the organisation's growth rate and the level of technology the company is engaged in. For example, if you are a stable long-term organisation dealing in long lead times (say, electricity generation), the performance drivers will be quite different from those that apply to newspaper or periodical publishing. Performance drivers also embrace the cultural conditions in which you operate. This is particularly important, as culture may get in the way of change and a clear understanding of culture will tell you how appropriate any suggested practices are to your organisation. It is sensible to analyse the performance drivers that apply to your organisation in a manner such as that set out in Table 38. Of course, these are only examples but they should illustrate the point of the exercise, which is to match yourself with a comparator who can add something to how you see yourself. Of course, 'best-practice' is subjective and transitory, and this fits neatly into the fluid framework of HR. The search for a high-quality product that meets customers' needs is a perpetual journey – not a destination. Even while a high-quality product is being delivered successfully to approving customers, an HR quality organisation will be implementing the next improvement.

Benchmarking clubs and organisations

One way of developing partners is to use the variety of clubs that are now becoming available in a response to the need to finding benchmarking partners. Most of the consultants listed in Appendix 2 have access to firms who will happily join up with your organisation. These organisations also have access to databases that will be particularly useful. The consultancies have people who specialise in HR matters. There is, in addition, 'The Best-Practice Club' which again can put your organisation in touch with partners in the areas of interest to you.

Such organisations can be very valuable in helping your organisation get quick access to data, but obviously they can be expensive. The connections and the related data have been put together at a cost, and you must pay for it. It is also important to recognise that a consultancy does not just want to sell you data, they also wish to sell their expertise so that they can help you get the best out of the data.

Informal discussion groups

There is a way of developing partners for benchmarking that can be easily overlooked. In joining an informal best-practice club meeting that takes place (eg the Phoenix Club, available

Table 40

BENCHMARKING AWAYDAYS:
TOUGH HR ISSUES RAISED

The balance between work and life
- ☐ Are we expecting too much of our people?
- ☐ Are they working late because they enjoy it?
- ☐ Are families being neglected by breadwinners working away?
- ☐ Is there any evidence one way or the other?

Technology and the structure of jobs
- ☐ How flexible can people be?
- ☐ What happens to the less able? – the unemployable?
- ☐ Flexibility – is it enriching? How generalist can you become?
- ☐ Can shift rotas and annualised hours be changed/introduced?

Process management
- ☐ If we devolve training, who will invent the next change in technology?
- ☐ Will HR people fit into a line structure?
- ☐ Will managers be responsible or abuse freedoms?

Rewards
- ☐ Can we change our grades and incremental systems?
- ☐ Can we persuade employees and unions it is better?
- ☐ Can we just reward competences gained and performance?
- ☐ What of the contractual position?

Empowerment and responsibility
- ☐ End of job titles?
- ☐ Can we really trust our people?
- ☐ What happens if it goes wrong?

to customers of one consultant; see Appendix 2) it is possible to get in on the ground floor of changes that are taking place. There is no reason why you should not invite a small group of like-minded people to join your own benchmarking club. Through such groups you can get at many key issues for your organisation and discuss them in a frank and open way. An example of the type of material emerging from such an away-day is given in Table 40. Such issues are raised in a non-threatening environment. Subjects that can hardly be spoken of in the company have an opportunity of an airing. In this case the company was concerned about the effect on people's lives of the changes taking place. Another concern was flexibility and what happened to employees who could not adapt. The fears of decentralising HR, the possible changes to shift rotas and the introduction of annualised hours, the problems of a rigid grading structure – all these and many more issues can be discussed. Many people have found this sort of group to be particularly useful.

It is essential that you are clear about what you might get from different prospective partners. It is possible to use first-level benchmarking to identify areas that might need attention. The discussion group with your partners can then be used by the benchmarking team to consider and reflect on various possible actions and find out how better-performing organisations have handled similar situations. Discussion groups of this nature that are specifically directed at benchmarking partners are proving very useful. You might consider using professional bodies to provide such a forum. Local IPD branches, for example, will be more than willing to develop existing networks into benchmarking clubs to discuss best practice. By reading professional magazines it is possible to identify possible 'best practices' being implemented by organisations. The group can then invite such organisations to consider them as benchmarking partners. Where this can be done on an informal and off-the-record basis, rather than in the formality of a conference setting, everyone will gain more from it.

Have the partners got data?

It will be apparent when you commence benchmarking, and invite a few prospective partners or consultants to come and see you, that there is an enormous amount of data available. The explosion of networking information technology has made such developments possible. Information that was once locked in documentation can now be made freely available. The internet and electronic mail have become a source of transfer for such information. There are now so many databases that there are databases of databases!

Managers are rightly sceptical of the metrics providing any immediate solution, but it is an important consideration when selecting partners. It is crucial to understand the impact of changes on employees, trade unions, customers and suppliers. It is necessary to think through the political implications of change and decide whether the medicine is worse than the disease. The problem is not whether the data exist but how they might be efficiently accessed and whether the partner you are considering also has access to them. You do not want the flow of data to be all one way.

One obvious problem is the decay that sets in the moment information is reported – is it up to date? You must have partners who understand the problem and are able to put resources into updating information. This is a particular problem the more you attempt to benchmark small or detailed parts of an organisation. The obvious example is in relation to comparing HR staff numbers with other organisations. On close investigation it may be that productivity improvement staff are included in your figures, whereas in the benchmark they are not. Labour turnover analyses are another area fraught with problems because it is known that labour turnover is strongly related to length of service. If the organisation or department has recently engaged in a recruitment exercise then its labour turnover will tend to be high. That is why survival rates are a much more valid indicator of organisational well-being, but they are not generally available and therefore cannot be benchmarked. It is also as well to remember that just because information is in a benchmarking database that does not make it correct or relevant. Your partners must be willing to spend some time going over the data and looking at the processes they relate to and be committed to keeping them up to date.

Summary and conclusion

This chapter has looked at the issues that emerge when the time comes to select partners for your benchmarking project. First you must have an analysis of your own organisation, as in this way the subsequent exercise will be more meaningful. You can benchmark internal units – particularly if you are part of a large group – but most users will eventually look to competitors or industry or generic partners. Partners can be found through the formal clubs, but you are encouraged to investigate self-help groups both to provide data and also to reflect on new ways of doing things. Also, do not ignore all the other listed sources of data. It is in these ways that you can identify best practice and seek to meet or better it. But remember – best practice is transitory. It is a useful notion but not one to be treated like the Holy Grail!

9

A STRATEGIC ROLE FOR HUMAN RESOURCE DEPARTMENTS

What this chapter offers

This book is written primarily for managers of people, whether they are line managers or functional managers with special responsibility for people issues. They are both, however, groups that can provide the ingredient missing from much of benchmarking activity – a consideration of the human issues.

This chapter addresses two aspects – both are important but the second holds considerably greater promise for the HR activity. First, what will be suggested is that it is possible to have a strategy for managing the resources within the HR department itself. Second, it is possible to involve the HR unit in the development of an HR strategy for the organisation itself. Both can be assisted by benchmarking. The comparisons inherent in benchmarking can be used as pointers to where change might be made. HR benchmarks of performance can be established in areas such as learning and training, absence, recruitment, employee development and reward management.

Managing the HR function strategically

One of the important benefits of benchmarking is that it helps to establish what your customers think of the service you are offering, and then allows you to set benchmarks for improvement. Personnel has traditionally been cast in the lead role of organisation 'nay-sayers' – the department that likes to say no, presumably stemming from the power derived in many organisations by personnel units from their relations with trade unions. Unfortunately, it is rarely the case that trade union relations are based on change, growth and a proactive approach to solving problems. In areas of conflict and contract it is usually easier to say no than to take the risks inherent in saying yes.

It is a brave idea in benchmarking to give managers a questionnaire and ask them what they think of the personnel/HR function and the service it provides. It takes courage to risk the criticism of fellow managers (most of whom would not risk a similar exercise in respect of their own departments!). This was the idea behind just such an exercise set out in Chapter 3. It is also essential to involve HR staff in a separate study of their aims and objectives. It is important that questionnaires look at two aspects:

- [ ] the importance of an activity
- [ ] the level of performance achieved.

This can be drawn schematically, as shown in Figure 9. Such an approach is particularly useful for the HR function. There is always a risk that the department is engaged on tasks that are not seen as central to the operation of the business, or which do not increase asset value. The general idea would be to reduce the time spent on any activities that come out in segment D and conversely increase the attention given to tasks emerging in segments B and A. The argument is that there is little point achieving high performance in a low priority area (therefore recorded as D). Meanwhile, important areas that have a poor level of performance need urgent attention and are classed in Figure 9 as B.

It could be argued that high performing areas classed as 'C' should continue – why reduce performance? The answer is that there is always pressure on resources. Resources that are spent on activities in area 'C' (canteens, and sports and social clubs?) cannot be spent elsewhere. The good people who are performing well on those tasks could sensibly be moved to other, more important, tasks in areas B or A. This is always a difficult choice and one that is frequently avoided. Stopping doing your favourite tasks – or perhaps even more unpopularly, the

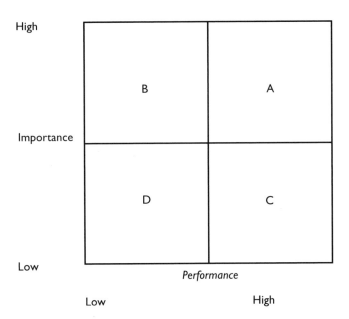

Figure 9

DESIGNING SURVEYS:
Importance v Performance

favourite tasks of your staff – is always difficult, but it is just this sort of issue that benchmarking will bring out.

Comparing assessments of importance

In providing answers to questions it is always useful to analyse results in terms of the importance that you attach to a subject, and compare that with the importance a 'customer' attaches to it. The resulting chart can look something like Figure 10, which is drawn from a Newcastle-based marketing company. The information can be obtained by asking managers to complete a benchmarking questionnaire, as in this particular case. The questionnaire simply asks managers to give their views on the HR department's activities and to rate them according to a scale. The results from the survey are then compared graphically as a chart, as shown in Figure 10. It is also possible to derive the information without using the

Figure 10

YOUR IMPORTANCE *V* OUR IMPORTANCE

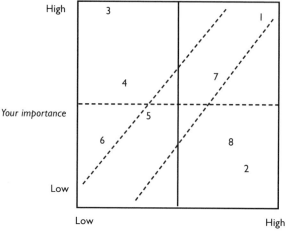

1 = employee negotiations
2 = management development
3 = employee handbooks
4 = recruitment
5 = canteens
6 = social clubs
7 = productivity schemes
8 = job evaluation

formality of a questionnaire. In this approach the same sort of questions can be asked at a seminar. In both cases the manager's results are compared with the opinions of the HR department. Finally, these results can be compared with outside organisations to determine the external benchmark of performance.

It might be thought that the ideal outcome would be to set a benchmark in the central dotted band area, and work towards achieving that. This would imply that there was unanimity of agreement of purpose on what was important. Since these managers are your 'customers' you must, of course, respond to their needs. You would therefore work to meet their aspirations for up-to-date publications (no. 3) but would you spend less time and effort on management development (no. 2) and job evaluation (no. 8) because the managers assess these items as having a low priority? It has to be remembered that benchmarking is not an exact science even when the numbers come with such a strong pedigree as here (after all, what can be better than meeting your 'customer's' needs). In this case perhaps managers are expressing displeasure at the way the organisation approaches management development and job evaluation, rather than rejecting the idea of a strategy directed at such matters. Whatever the reason it is not good enough to abdicate responsibility by saying ' this is what my customers want' .

Understanding what 'customer' means

There is a danger in the suggestion that the ' personnel' department has customers. First, although the idea of an HR department 'selling' its services has been tried by some companies (IDS report 1997), there can be something false about it. What is wrong is that the 'customer' usually does not have much choice. The line department is not free to refuse those services and go elsewhere. The notion of markets and customers requires freedom of choice. Some organisations have gone further and established supposedly independent external services. The problem is that a few have at the same time manipulated the prices charged, so that a totally unrealistic market exists. At this point many organisations have become so frustrated that they have outsourced huge areas of their common services. This often appears to be the only way of stopping the waste that seems to arise when there is no true competition. This has resulted in many HR functions being totally devolved and with them perhaps the hope for a sensible understanding and formulation of the strategic people issues.

In Figure 10 the HR department (it was a personnel department at the time) accepted criticism regarding the lack of importance it attached to 'handbooks'. These were management's 'bibles' of rules and regulations and were hopelessly out of date. The reality, of course, was that it is always easy to ignore the mundane, to miss out the detail. The personnel department knew that managers wanted 'handbooks' but no one wanted to be bothered with them – how could they therefore admit to their importance!

This was not the situation in respect of management development (no. 2) and job evaluation (no. 8). The result was a major review of what was the purpose of development and job evaluation. It transpired that what managers were critical of was not the ideas and principles underlying those activities but the bureaucratic and time-consuming method of their implementation.

Benchmarking the HR department

The advantage of undertaking benchmarking of the HR department is that it is possible to achieve much by asking managers what they expect. Following an analysis and challenge of expectations, benchmarks can be set and worked towards. All this can be done internally and within your own time and resources. While a benchmarking team is required and managers have to support the initiative (particularly if they are to be asked to complete questionnaires) the exercise is considerably lower key than an external attempt at benchmarking.

Affecting what managers do

There are some points to make about benchmarking in this way within the HR department. While some matters can be handled with the department, some cannot be changed without the agreement and support of other managers. This is, of course, true of all departments, but perhaps it applies particularly to HR.

Some items such as reducing costs, improving accuracy and shortening time-scales can perhaps be handled internally. However, even these areas will need the support of managers if the HR organisation is to change, or if documentation is to be revised or procedures changed. For example, benchmarking may have highlighted concern about delays in recruitment. You may recognise that hand-offs and authorisation steps can be reduced to speed up the recruitment process by eliminating some stages and integrating others (the recruitment process given in Chapter 5 is an example of this). It is therefore necessary and important that some element of discussion with colleagues takes place.

One purpose of benchmarking is to facilitate the identification and implementation of 'best practice'. It will therefore be necessary in analysing how the HR unit might improve its performance to benchmark against external companies or organisations. This need not be as difficult as it sounds. Using the variety of benchmarking clubs and self-help approaches discussed in the last chapter, it is possible to undertake benchmarking without incurring either great effort or expense.

Benchmarking for the HR department will have four areas to be looked at. These are:

☐ organisational issues
☐ roles and responsibilities
☐ HR processes
☐ individual competences.

Organisational issues

This is the opportunity to undertake routine and basic analysis as to how the HR organisation is operating. This will involve internally surveying managers and external contacts to help establish the most appropriate benchmark. This analysis will include primary-level benchmarking with other companies, covering employment (number of HR employees/1,000 whole company employees), absence (days lost for office workers and factory/outside employees) accidents and labour turnover, pay and benefits. Recruitment costs and time taken to recruit new people are further areas that should be benchmarked. The number of trainers employed and the training days/training employee will identify their level of efficiency benchmarked with other organisations.

Organisational issues would also include obvious matters such as structure and relationships. Are there any inherent weaknesses in how the department is structured (but not covering any individual strengths and weaknesses). For example, problems can occur if development is not part of training, or medical matters are not part of HR services.

Roles and responsibilities and time allocated

It is also essential to address roles and responsibilities. This will include the share of time and resources allocated to a particular area of work. You may have excellent departments in training, occupational health, recruitment and so on. If you decide you need to sharpen up on employee development or equal opportunities you may have to decide priorities. It is always difficult to stop doing work that you do well. The test must always be whether it is a task that managers want, and which has some direct effect on the core business. If not, there must be a doubt as to whether that work should continue.

Analysis of HR processes

This leads to an analysis of HR procedures. It is necessary to test out changes with the users. The point has already been made that the HR department is rarely the controller of its own destiny in such matters. The author has never encountered an HR department that could not benefit from an overhaul of a number of its important processes. Included for first-level benchmarking would be recruitment, development and appraisal, job evaluation and training. It would also be correct to include employee relations, but there has to be a recognition of what might or might not be possible. Without a fundamental strategically focused overhaul there will be no motivation for trade unions to change.

Competences

We need to benchmark competences, skills and capabilities. In general terms the issue is whether benchmarking can identify shortcomings in your staff that need additional training to rectify. Perhaps they have not kept competences up to date, which can soon be rectified. Perhaps there are significant numbers of HR staff without line management skills and therefore with an insufficient understanding of a line manager's problems. This may be a factor identified from the surveys. Many of the criticisms of HR stem from a belief that HR is 'not part of the real world'. It is possible that when you undertake an analysis of competences, areas such as inadequate planning, lack of business focus or slowness in decision-making are raised by respondents. These are all areas that can be dealt with, at least in part, by a training and development approach. It is possible that some swapping of employees with line departments will aid the understanding and performance of both considerably. It is always surprising how few HR people have ever done other jobs. It is a weakness that need not be tolerated.

Towards a strategy for HR

These practices are excellent if you are satisfied with the overall function and you have no desire or motivation to move to something different. Many HR units have neither the resources nor the individual competences to move into areas of HR strategy or to become internal HR consultants. It is natural and right for them to carry out what they are doing well, and try to make improvements of the type referred to above.

To change obviously requires the building of HR credibility. How might that be done? It is to those who already have a responsibility in the strategic area and wish to sharpen up their practice of it, that the remainder of this chapter and Chapter 10 are directed. There have always been people in personnel management who have pressed for the involvement of HR in strategic issues. This is partly about self-respect and self-interest as a profession. A responsibility for strategy carries with it a seat on the board, or at least influence over the chief executive officer (CEO). In earlier times that influence was derived from HR's special abilities to handle employee relations. Although that aspect has waned for many companies it is still a source of strength, and will perhaps be again. The problem for HR is that the negativism of much industrial relations is the antithesis of what human resource strategies should be about.

Defining HR strategy

What, then, do we mean by, or expect from, an HR strategy? There are those who use terms like vision, strategy, focus, resources, development, planning, rewards and the rest. If you wish, it is possible to play a game with such 'strategy' words. Simply take a long list of them and go through them at random throwing in the odd verb. The ease with which impressive sounding sentences are thrown up should worry the reader. This is the problem with much of the work of the excellent Personnel Standards Lead Body (PSLB), now renamed the Occupational Standards Council. In defining the work of the HR department it said the intention of HR was to:

> 'Develop and maintain an appropriate personnel strategy to support the overall strategy of the organisation.'

and

> 'Enable the creation of an organisation structure and work processes that maximise the performance of people at work to deliver the organisations strategy'.

or

> 'Contribute to the overall strategy of the organisation by providing generalist and specialist information and advice'.

Such statements cannot be improved upon. (Individuals would not agree with that, but whether they could get others to agree with their changes must be doubted!). Such statements are, of course, committee compromises – and they have to be. The problem is that they are like 'motherhood and apple pie' – we all agree with them. The test in this context is whether they help a non-strategist to move towards a strategic view of HR.

The danger of benchmarking 'best practice' in HR terms is that an individual organisation's best activities are chosen, which do not link together into a coherent whole. What happens is that an excellent absence control procedure is copied but not the support and counselling that makes it work. A process-managed development procedure that applies to all employees is emulated, but it does not work well because the value of trust that enables it to work is not in place. There is no sense of strategy as piecemeal attempts at improvement are made. The problem of such statements as those above, that commonly form organisational strategies, is that they help only those who know what the strategy is in the first place.

A further point is that details determine what a strategy looks like; the details determine the outcome. Not for nothing did the philosopher remark that the 'devil is in the detail'. This is why benchmarking is so useful in forming an HR strategy. It is possible to reflect on organisations that have spent months looking at HR strategy. Pages of worthy statements have been prepared; presentations have been made; conferences addressed; training courses attended, and yet the impact on strategic HR has been nil. The people who were influencing strategy may have recognised that strategy comes from a sharply focused vision of what the organisation is about, but they are less likely to understand the importance of detail. Every action is judged against that end. As long as you have a secure vision simply expressed, then detail leads automatically to the strategy. Setting out a strategy in terms of statements like those above will not lead to strategic HR. The strategy is the result of the study of detail measured against the organisation's vision and values. To start from strategy without reference to what is happening on the ground is to court cynicism. This leads to the 'stated policy' in which the organisation grandly expresses views on what it wants to happen, but that is then compared by employees with the 'done policy' – which is what actually happens on the ground. The employees often see the differences.

Summary and conclusion

This chapter has considered the benchmarking of the HR department itself. It has stressed four areas of benchmarking, namely organisational issues, roles and responsibilities, individual competences and HR processes themselves. By using measurement approaches such as questionnaires and metrics it is possible to compare how the organisation is doing in any particular HR area. You can measure any matter, whether it be absence rates, labour turnover, or recruitment times and costs. If, however, you are seeking to benchmark a strategy for HR that makes a difference to the organisation, the next chapter is the place to look.

10

BENCHMARKING HUMAN RESOURCE STRATEGIES IN PRACTICE

What this chapter is about

In the last chapter it was suggested that there is a role for the HR professional beyond managing the HR department. This chapter deals with HR strategies that go beyond a narrow view of HR and into areas of business results. For example, a manager might say that whether he has a commission scheme for the sales staff is up to him or her. However, a commission scheme affects how people are paid and how they see themselves and how the organisation deals with them. To tackle a manager over such a matter is a hopeless task for HR unless there is an agreed reward strategy against which it can be measured. This is an important role and one that goes beyond merely giving advice. The business of people is too important for a detached professional advisory role. The HR department could be at the very heart of events – some would even say the centre of a battle – although most HR professionals would probably say 'at the point of discussion'! This chapter deals with those strategic issues that go beyond the activities of HR and become matters that affect the whole organisation.

The position of some HR people in the organisation hierarchy does not always permit them to exercise the kind of power that these strategies require. Some other organisations do not have an HR department at all. In that situation this chapter is directed at whoever is responsible for formulating the more or less explicit people policies of the organisation. Conversely, some organisations have HR departments that have a seat on the main 'board' or very near to it. For them the exercise of power is an easier option.

HR and benchmarking

What is suggested is a two-pronged approach. First, the task is to ensure that people issues are considered at the top of the organisational agenda. Second, the intention is gradually to change the way the organisation thinks about employees and the policies that it has to deal with people issues. These aspects are not, of course, separate; they complement each other. The way to achieve the first is usually through strategies for the second.

Not for the first time have people policies seemed in the ascendant. It happened in the mid-1960s and parts of the 1970s, but it really gained hold in the later 1980s. There were signs that managers had begun to appreciate that good people actions would have a positive effect. The idea of organisations having vision and values in the 1980s began to show some hope that significant change was taking place. Benchmarking has emerged as a major way that companies can avoid the slow pace of evolutionary change. The fear and threat of competition and the need for management to meet customers' requirements – and often restructure their organisations as a result – has alarmed some commentators. Step changes become possible and are achieved. However, earlier benchmarking had a tendency to an overly technical approach and forgot people. The opportunity to overcome that earlier weakness arises now that HR is becoming part of the reviewing and benchmarking process. This idea of reviewing the HR function is explored and developed in Fonda and Buckton 1995.

HR strategy in practice

Words like strategy, scenario, plans and the rest are in common currency. But what is meant by an 'HR strategy' and how is it different from actions that do not form a strategy? First, an HR strategy does not exist simply because there is a long and complex document entitled 'An HR strategy for xyz company'.

Table 41

ELEMENTS THAT MAKE AN HR STRATEGY

☐	There must be clearly defined goals.
☐	It is essential to have well-understood intentions of behaviour.
☐	Operations and detailed actions must follow the strategic direction.
☐	Results must be achievable over a period of time.
☐	Policies must be linked together to form a coherent pattern.
☐	Policies must be mutually supporting and avoid contrary tensions.
☐	HR strategy must be supportive of corporate aims and results.
☐	There must be a facility for evaluation, feedback and review.

Examples of such documents abound and they are as much use as many of the manpower and corporate plans of the 1960s and 1970s. They had little beneficial impact on company practice.

What features should a strategy have? The items in Table 41 are suggested. The idea of goals is important, as you must know where you are hoping to go. The aspect of behaviour refers to corporate behaviour, that is how the organisation will deal with any particular circumstances that arise. This leads to the operational tactics and how the organisation is managed on a day-to-day basis. All policy must be linked together to form a coherent framework to be achieved in full over a period of time. Related to this is that all policy and individual actions must be mutually supportive, with an emphasis on the avoidance of conflicting tensions. The policy must link through to business results where priorities are set, key problems identified and plans established to meet them. The delivery of results is where the detailed management of day-to-day practices comes in, with decisions being measured against policy to minimise conflict between the actions taking place and the policy itself. It is essential that the strategy has within it a facility for evaluation and feedback so that problems can be debated and performance improved. These key elements and the criteria against which they are measured are set out in Table 42.

Table 42

EVALUATING STRATEGY

The process area	Measured against
Vision	☐ defining goals: what sort of organisation are we? what is the organisational purpose?
Policy formulation	☐ turning vision to practical policy ☐ linked coherent policies ☐ policies that do not compete
Deciding key results	☐ identification of the key organisational drivers ☐ establishment of achievability periods ☐ deciding on priorities ☐ key problems ☐ key opportunities and shortcomings ☐ financial performance ☐ product and customer services ☐ innovation and a healthy organisation
Delivery of results	☐ detailed management of day-to-day practices ☐ learning, training and retraining ☐ performance management ☐ balanced scorecard measurement ☐ practices measured against policy
Benchmarking	☐ how we did ☐ evaluation and feedback ☐ areas to be improved ☐ areas doing better
Feedback	☐ listening to employees ☐ listening to managers and customers ☐ impact of detail debated with managers ☐ review and update of policies.

The importance of HR strategy in benchmarking

In practical terms these principles have to be turned into a
coherent HR strategy for the organisation. The danger of
benchmarking in this environment is that HR *à la carte* is not
the way to construct an HR strategy. You may look at what
other organisations do and see that they achieve lower costs
than are achieved in your organisation. There may be a

temptation to reduce training manpower because the bench-marked organisation does much better than yours. Or you introduce executive health care because comparator firm finds it attractive and it seems to work. Perhaps you like what you see of teamwork and you start to implement that. However, you are concerned about the lack of clear decisions or rules on who can introduce a change in response to a customer's request. So job descriptions are introduced with clear and specific rules and controls defining who does what. The conflict should be apparent. How can you encourage teamwork and innovation in a closely controlled environment ruled by job descriptions?

The list is endless. If benchmarking *à la carte* is done in that way then no strategy can exist. The organisation will continue, like many others in HR, with no attempt to understand the conflicts inherent within the various tactical and strategic approaches. In Table 43 a list is drawn up of some of these contrasting policies. It is fashionable to imply that somewhere near list A is the only place to be. That is not the argument being put forward here. Whether you go towards list A, list B or some other list, the strategic policies – and just as impor-tant, the detailed day-to-day actions – must not conflict with one another. This is why detail is so important in assessing strategy because it is in the detail that strategy is brought to life. Visions, strategies and policies may be formulated in week-long conferences in fine hotels with excellent facilities, but that does not result in the organisation having an HR strat-egy. What counts is every decision that is taken every day – that is where strategy comes from.

Benchmarking for HR strategies

In benchmarking terms, this concentration on detail is neces-sary because benchmarking compares discrete items. Consider, as an example, the position with employee benefits. A map can be constructed of each individual practice that takes place in the organisation that affects benefits. Each one of the categori-sations (eg death and injury, absence, sickness and pregnancy benefits) is then measured against its cost (can we afford what we have, or do we need to reduce costs?) and against the strate-

Table 43

DRAWING UP AN HR STRATEGY:
SOME EXAMPLES OF EXTREMES

List A	List B
☐ empowerment	☐ control and restriction
☐ learning organisation	☐ training for the job only
☐ reward-based performance	☐ little performance management
☐ trust	☐ everything documented
☐ wide responsibility	☐ responsibility restricted to job
☐ 360-degree programmes for all employees	☐ executive 360-degree programmes
☐ 'can do' culture	☐ action controlled by rules
☐ mutually supportive/teamwork	☐ managed individuals
☐ no status divisions	☐ status cars/dining
☐ healthcare to all at cost	☐ executive free healthcare
☐ general policy decides employee dealings	☐ detailed TU rules and agreements
☐ employee development	☐ management development
☐ employee benefit programme	☐ status-directed benefit programme
☐ focus on equal opportunities and harassment issues	☐ actions limited to policy statements and dealing with breaches
☐ broadbanding pay measurement	☐ grades with steps – little room for manoeuvre
☐ communication and feedback	☐ information provided on a 'need to know' basis
☐ redeployment, retraining and structured severance.	☐ redundancy the normal option state-level redundancy payments only.

gic framework to determine whether the item meets or enhances the vision, or is its effect negative?

This is the approach to follow when benchmarking HR strategies. Reward strategies should include discussions about incremental progression and gradings. Broadbanding, for example, is a popular way of introducing performance measurement into reward systems. But it is not possible to leave it there; there are other issues to consider. Do managers have sufficient understanding of jobs to fit in with broadbanding? Are our job competences set out? If they are, how measurable are the criteria? Has the organisation a history of measurement of jobs and performance to give some confidence that broadbanding can be managed in practice?

In looking at HR organisational relationships, benchmarking will identify some organisations that transfer HR operations to line managers. It is possible to keep the 'dotted line' relationship and it may be helpful for a while. The dotted line is supposed to represent not quite direct managerial control but the possibility of exerting some sort of formal influence. The question to consider is why that 'comfort blanket' of apparent control is necessary, with the obvious implication that the line manager is not trusted. For a short period while the transfer beds in it may be sensible, but not thereafter. Consider the position of law and accounting – do they have dotted lines running throughout the organisation? For this author a dotted line is a sign of a unit that is unsure of itself and its position. It is important to remember that managing an organisation is not about charts. They are rarely other than poor reflections of practical relationship networks.

What of employee relations? The proposal is to package off the administrative routines and transactional services. What remains will be proactive decision-making, guiding and consulting. Perhaps employee relations is different. The problem is that a minor problem can become something of organisation-stopping proportions. How feasible is it to pass down all employee relations activities? There is the risk that managers will, under pressure, make agreements that conflict with the central policy. The spectre of a myriad pay rates for similar jobs is not a tempting prospect. If the day-to-day aspects can be handled you still need a facility to allow appeals to higher authority within the organisation. Also, pay negotiations, even if guided by a team of line managers, need strong HR support and not a little direction. For these sorts of politicised roles this author believes there remains a case to retain a reactive service HR unit that deals with such problems.

There is, of course, no dividing line between vision, strategy, policy and day-to-day decisions. They are all essential – and without them all you do not have a strategy. Most organisations will find that benchmarking requires them to look at questions of reward because organisations that perform well almost universally have successful ways of linking reward to performance. Tying rewards to the measurement process makes things happen because it makes clear what really has to be done. Pay sharpens attention and provides focus. Those organisations that do not provide that focus are at a disadvantage. Those organisations with long pay scales and incremental progression cannot focus on performance as effectively as those organisations where pay is dependent on performance. It is possible to develop this theme by also relating pay to competences. The more competences people develop the more pay they receive. One organisation has stopped all pay increases except where they are related to gaining new competences. There are problems with these sorts of approaches to pay. What will the union reaction be to such proposals? Can the changes be afforded? No one is saying that such changes are easy. They all require the agreement of the participants in order to be implemented successfully, and this will take time. (For detailed discussion of the various types of reward strategy that can be followed, see Armstrong 1996.)

HR and benchmarking measurement

In these ways (and one could write a book on these issues alone) it is possible to benchmark HR strategy. This will result in an opportunity to identify problem areas where activities conflict with policy, or areas where policy does not exist at all. This is why HR must stake its claim to be the leader in HR strategy and why it is probably important to pass to line managers as many of the operational and process-supporting tasks as possible. Measurement is crucial to organisational performance and managers understand the limitations of a purely numerical approach. This is a good time for HR to be involved.

The 'balanced scorecard' type of approach provides the sort of measurement system that seeks to embrace all facets of the organisation's objectives (Kaplan and Norton 1993). The scorecard includes customers, financial measures, innovation and employee issues. If tested more, and internalised within the performance and measurement process, there is hope that HR values and beliefs can be turned into the coherent strategic HR framework that organisations need: a framework that embraces hard measures such as financial control budgets, earnings per share and return on investment along with innovation, learning and the creation of a healthy organisation. This sort of benchmarked analysis can be undertaken for all aspects of HR work and used to develop an HR strategy. (For detailed discussion of HR strategies, see Marchington and Wilkinson 1996.)

Summary and conclusion

This chapter has discussed HR strategy. It is suggesting an involvement in benchmarking that goes beyond the confines of the HR department and affects those matters that are seen as purely business, but nevertheless have a significant impact on people. To summarise, why do you need a strategy? It is necessary to make the organisation a pleasant, trustworthy and business results-oriented place to work. Without a strategy decisions will change randomly, depending on who made them and how they felt at the time. An HR strategy is not just writing out a lot of fine-sounding words on a piece of paper. Of course that is important, but it must go beyond that and into affecting each decision made on a day-to-day basis.

11

PILOTING BENCHMARKING
IN PRACTICE

How do we start?

This chapter deals with the practical steps you should consider when contemplating a benchmarking pilot. It is necessary to be clear in your own mind where you stand within the organisation. Are you the managing director or chief executive officer? Are you a director or a departmental manager? You must assess your position in the organisation realistically. If you lack the necessary power to get things done you have to accept the reality and act accordingly. If you try to implement benchmarking beyond the limit of your power and without the necessary support, you will not succeed. Even worse, you could stop someone else taking action who *is* in a position to carry benchmarking through.

You might, for example, decide to recognise the need to start with a low key approach and introduce benchmarking in your own department. You can still make significant progress but you lessen the risk of over reaching yourself. You can also prepare the ground for the future by reporting your initiative to a meeting of managers and referring to it as a pilot or trial. This is an excellent way of getting support, particularly if you use it to review issues in your own department.

Establishing a pilot

Table 44 lists some considerations for establishing a pilot benchmarking exercise. We considered the question of your power to act in the preceding section, but you must also understand your own motivation. Are you simply looking to check

Table 44

MANAGING BENCHMARKING IN PRACTICE: AGREEING A PILOT

☐   What is your motivation?

☐   Are you willing to fight for the benefits of benchmarking?

☐   Have you the power?

   – Recognise your limitations and work within them.

   – Support is crucial to a project.

☐   Establish a trial/pilot exercise.

   – Use your own department.

   – Show a readiness to change yourself.

☐   Report the setting up of a trial.

   – Report regularly on progress.

that everything is in order, or are you aware of problems? Do you perceive that the problems are organisation wide? Do you regard this exercise as the first stage before the bigger issues can be reviewed? Answers to all of these questions will affect how you progress.

In any event, if benchmarking is an HR-led activity it is sensible to start at home with any pilot or trial. It is not sensible for an HR manager to be criticising other managers' fiefdoms when there are problems for all to see in the HR department which are not being dealt with. It may be possible to make early progress and change some of those aspects for which you are distrusted and disliked. Yours is an 'overhead' department, indirectly adding value to the organisation's assets, not to the product or service of the organisation. You are therefore in a weak position to criticise other managers who are generating revenue or dealing directly with customers. You may know of possible early wins for the benchmarking exercise. Perhaps benchmarking will suggest that one of your sections is much larger than is generally felt necessary. If so, you can take steps to reduce it. Perhaps absence control is poor and HR inhibits rather than facilitates its management. Then take the initiative to change it. Your recruitment process may be interminably long – shorten it! Your training department may have a reputation as a 'happy-valley' – sharpen it up. Perhaps your agreements and guidance notes are out of date. You can update them. These are some of the common complaints that exist against HR. You need to identify those that are relevant to your own situation and deal with them. People will accept change much more readily when they see your willingness to challenge some of your own departmental beliefs.

Consultants in the pilot?

Some suggested steps for running a pilot are given in Table 45. Some of the key issues from that list will now be considered. You will have to decide one important issue – will you have consultant support for the pilot? There is clearly a case for involving them from the start, particularly if you intend that the organisation will move on to bigger things in the future. You have to think through this matter with care. You will need support if the organisation becomes committed to large-scale benchmarking. Consultants also are useful in providing an external reference point. The organisation will accept ideas from a consultant that could be seen as politically motivated if offered by an internal manager.

A problem arises if you do not manage the consultant and ensure that he or she keeps to your agenda and cost. The project must be fully scoped by this stage. It is essential that the role of the consultant is clear to you both, together with an understanding of when it will be reviewed. Any contractual issues regarding disengagement, such as the right to the use of material developed up to that stage, must be clear. Consultants often complain that they get inadequately briefed and they are therefore unable to help to their best ability. Thus, in the pilot these are some of the points you should be clear about:

- [ ] whether you have consultants at all
- [ ] whether you want low key general advice at this stage
- [ ] whether the consultant has access to more resources if the benchmarking project grows and you need more help.

Table 45

RUNNING A PILOT:

ISSUES TO CONSIDER

☐	Using consultants.
☐	Limiting the pilot project aims.
☐	Going for popular easy wins.
☐	Establishing a supervisory benchmarking group.
☐	Selecting a team leader and a team (they must be responsible for the task ie process owners).
☐	People impact.
☐	Selecting the pilot area for benchmarking.
☐	Selecting benchmarking partners.
☐	Building up support.
☐	Building up momentum.
☐	Making small incremental changes at first.

These are the sorts of questions you should be thinking about when you are arranging a pilot.

Limiting the aims of the pilot

In the pilot, whichever department is used it is important that benchmarking has full support among those who are directly involved. It will not succeed unless the managers of the unit or department involved are willing to give time and resources to benchmarking. This, of course, is the same for any project or activity.

Given that you have the support that is necessary, you need to think through the aims of the project. These have to be sufficiently simple that they can be managed within your own resources. This can, of course, include any resources that are given to you to complete a pilot. You may have the support of the CEO/MD (you may be the CEO/MD!) in which case the project can have bigger aims.

Whatever level of support you have, the point still applies to treat benchmarking in its pilot stages as having limited aims. The temptation must be avoided to rush at such matters and try to cover too much ground. This is a natural result of enthusiasm but can be damaging. If the pilot is seen to fail because it becomes overextended then dissatisfaction will set in. Managers who might have committed themselves willingly to a project following a successful pilot will inevitably be wary if benchmarking has failed. In conclusion, the recommendation is to achieve modest results with the possibility of achieving those results quickly and dramatically.

Establishing a supervisory group

Experience shows that, while you want to give the benchmarking team as much freedom as possible, it is also important that their work has somewhere to report to. The purpose is not to direct or control the day-to-day actions of the benchmarking team. It is important that the organisation knowledge-base about the opportunities and problems of benchmarking are shared. The problems and opportunities of benchmarking and the subsequent issues dealing with change will all be reinforced throughout the organisation by such a group if it is truly seen as representative of the organisation. At the very least, managers should be given the opportunity to take part.

The supervisory group should have as its leader/coach a senior director, or even the MD, who is committed to making benchmarking work. Its other members should reflect the power structure within the organisation. It should also, of course, include the pilot project team leader. The opportunity of overlap between the pilot team and any other teams established subsequently should not be overlooked. This will all lead to a strengthening and deepening of knowledge and experience of benchmarking and subsequent change.

Benchmarking teams and team leaders

It is often a good idea to allocate people to the benchmarking team on the basis of a period of secondment. Usually six to eight months is appropriate, depending on the nature, size and scope of the benchmarking project. At some stage, of course, it may become apparent that substantial change has to be made. The project will then become a long-term job like any other, even though it may be termed a 'project'. One successful approach, particularly as the concept takes hold, is to see the task as a tour of duty. Achievements gained while in the benchmarking team will become part of the manager's balanced scorecard and developing competences. In an organisation that manages development properly the candidate will not be 'seconded' from the 'contractual task' and then returned to it after the period of the attachment. The opportunity should be taken to institute continuous development, at least for some high-flying employees. The attachment to the benchmarking project then becomes one of a number of competence-building steps in a career. In this way of thinking there is no sense of leaving a job and then going back to it. The person may be continually moving, adding to behavioural and skill competences in a significant way.

An important point is that the team leader should be someone who owns the problem – who will feel the problems if it fails. All too often team leadership (of any project, not just benchmarking) is given to someone in the authority structure who is not directly involved in the process being benchmarked. Even worse – even if entirely well intentioned, responsibility is given to what should be seen as a specialist support service, not a decision owner/taker. Far too many projects have been given to planning managers, or productivity managers. A 1990s version of the same mistake would be to allocate a TQM manager or the organisation's quality expert, or business focus improvement manager, or change manager or whatever. If we remember the advice given in Chapter 5, the person in charge should be a 'process manager', that is someone who is in charge of the process being measured and compared.

All support should be available either strategically through a supervisory group or operationally through the pilot team. It is more important that the project team itself should consist of people who have a strong desire to follow up any decision to extend benchmarking. There is little point having a member whose department is deeply sceptical. At this early stage the project will need support and it will not help to have sniping from within. There will be plenty of time and opportunity to bring on board those who are less committed to benchmarking.

Selecting the pilot benchmarking area

This is a very important issue: too big an agenda and benchmarking will fail; too minor an issue and there will be no impact. Apart from that, people involved must understand benchmarking and be willing to go along with the intentions of it in the department or unit under investigation. These issues are set out in Table 46. The pilot should be undertaken by a department that is willing. It might be a department where there is a problem of some importance to the company. Some companies have chosen HR projects because of the spread of their work across all other departments.

Therefore, for example, if you decide to benchmark recruitment and selection, that is a subject in which all managers and departments have a key interest, although it will be owned (at least in its strategic aspects) by the HR department. If you are looking at the operational aspects of selection rather than the more strategic issues of recruitment, it may be helpful to have a line manager leading the pilot group. You have to recognise, of course, that if you decide to make changes in the recruitment and selection procedures, then you will almost certainly have to make some similar changes across the whole organisation. The project will also gain if the pilot area is something

Table 46

SELECTING THE PILOT AREA

☐	The unit has to be a willing participant.
☐	It has to have lessons that can be shared.
☐	It has to be a subject that other managers can relate to.
☐	It has to be relevant to all managers.
☐	It will be a bonus if all managers can gain from any early wins.
☐	Don't choose work that is commercially sensitive.

that managers can understand and relate to. If the subject for benchmarking is esoteric or walled in by confidentiality and security it is unlikely that other managers will gain much from the experience.

Selecting partners

This matter is discussed in detail in Chapter 8. It is essential that three to five good partners are chosen who are as enthusiastic as you are about the project. Perhaps they can be persuaded to join your own benchmarking group. It is possible, at least in the early stages, to select 'internal' partners. This is useful if you are part of a group of companies where access is relatively straightforward. There will be occasions when you can simply collect your benchmarking data from these units. It is therefore not absolutely essential that they are committed to benchmarking, as long as they are willing to provide some data for comparison purposes. A problem will arise, however, if you decide to look deeper into a problem. If partners are not committed to benchmarking they will be reluctant to have an in-depth study of a problem with you, perhaps regarding your efforts as a waste of time. It also has to be recognised that internal partners suffer or benefit from the same general culture as you do. In a benchmarking exercise carried out in one utility, although some of its companies were better than others in HR terms, all fared badly in the areas of costs and numbers employed, compared with the 'best in class' benchmarks derived externally.

Building up momentum and support

It should be a priority to build up momentum around the project. Some ideas are given in Table 47. The speed at which events happen is crucial. This is a difficult concept to get across. Why should it matter if something is done today rather than tomorrow if the circumstances are the same? What is lost? No deadlines for contracts are missed. No crucial purchase is delayed which can no longer be made. Why is momentum so important? If it is so important why do textbooks not make more of it?

Table 47

BUILDING MOMENTUM

☐ Explain benchmarking at major 'calling' conferences, workshops, etc.
☐ Explain the reasons – explain the benchmarking drivers.
☐ Get high-powered managers to give their support.
☐ Design a catchy slogan.
☐ Appoint credible people to the groups.
☐ Tell all your people about the early wins.
☐ Design and issue regular, brief and catchy reports.
☐ Issue quick reports on meetings.
☐ Think about benchmarking beer mats, pens, t-shirts – the lot!
☐ Work for employees' and union support – invite unions to the conferences.
☐ Encourage feedback and respond to it.
☐ Create an air of inevitability.
☐ Show concern and deal sensitively with any damage caused.
☐ Build trust and deserve it.

Above all, keep moving fast!

There are many people who will err on the side of the technical when describing organisations. They will talk of information technology, engineering, production, marketing and discounted cash flow. Any failure in the organisation will be seen as a failure of some system or other. Of course, systems do fail. But there is more to it than that. The difference between ordinary companies and good companies is the imaginative solutions and a willingness to dare to be different that gets things done. Every organisation has computer glitches, failures of procedure and human error – some organisations seem to have a team of people who willingly look at these problems. Momentum is needed in benchmarking because people are the key, and people need momentum to create enthusiasm and excitement. In this way a sense of drama is imparted and people sense they can enjoy this new project – they can have fun.

Organisations consist of people who will resist any attempt to reduce them to the technicalities. Momentum is the key way to overcome people's fear of, and consequent resistance to, the changes that are likely. If those changes are likely to affect people's jobs (and indeed whether they will have a job) the more likely is fear to be engendered and resistance increased. Many of the ideas in Table 47 may seem trivial. An organisation that is not used to humming with activity and the novel will be cynical about them. They may not all apply to, or be appropriate in, your circumstances but many organisations have created the momentum and support they were looking for with the use of such devices. For example, a memorable title for the project is essential. It should be something that is original to the organisation. Examples that have been tried are 'World Class by 2000', or 'Benchmarking is Special', another is 'Project Tooth – Tail'. (A navy reference to shifting people from support occupations to front-line duties.)

The people in the groups are particularly important. If those selected are seen as key players and high-fliers who are well placed in the organisation hierarchy, so much the better – other employees read the signals. If the project is organised by a person who has generally under performed, people will know what to think.

In order to build momentum you should plan to have regular eye-catching reports. Perhaps more important than the style is the time taken for something to be prepared and issued. With on-screen technology available to many managers and easy-to-use desk-top publishing equally usable by all, there is no reason why informative bulletins that are brief, interesting and to the point cannot be issued quickly.

It is very important that any progress made on identifying issues is quickly made available through such media. Any change – however small – that will be generally appreciated should be proclaimed loudly throughout the organisation and corporate headquarters! It is all part of a process that creates not only momentum but the feeling that change is coming and it cannot be stopped.

The opportunity should also be taken to explain what benchmarking is about. Perhaps a major conference with benchmarking as its theme is one approach. But this should be supported in other ways through workshops, training, courses, general updates, videos, house magazines and the rest.

Perhaps at the same time you should openly discuss the

possible changes that you are looking for, and that may result. You could invite an outside speaker from a partner organisation, who has some experience of benchmarking, to make a presentation to your employees. At this stage you have to show that you have a sensitivity to the human issues involved, and a caring concern for any casualties. You can do this by having in place a good commitment to a learning organisation. If all you have is a training centre perhaps you should look into what a 'learning organisation' might be and how employees and the organisation might benefit from it.

At the same time as considering such issues, it is important not to be talking only to the top slice of managers. Although they are important to making progress and providing political push, it is the employees who must implement any change. If you do not have their support then you will not succeed. One approach might be to treat employees as having an equal share in benchmarking. Organisations very commonly have included a wide cross-section of their people at such events. People must be properly briefed as to why they are attending, and so when they return to their units they can give feedback to their colleagues. It is important that people recognise their role as receivers and givers of information.

Another very important grouping who should be fully integrated into the processes and any conferences will be employee representative groups. In many cases this will be unions, where they are part of the company. They have a legitimate interest in understanding what is being done, and their support for any changes will be important. If they are doing their job well they will be able to express employees' fears and suggest solutions. It is regrettable that trade unions have gained a reputation for resisting change. They often appear to want to support the *status quo*. It is important to recognise that this is often a consequence of failing to understand the strategic drivers with which the organisation is dealing. If the organisation fails to share a debate about the strategic drivers with trade unions there should be no surprise when they do not support the consequences. In these ways you build momentum and support. Gradually the organisation becomes populated by people who embrace change and who will willingly seek its implementation.

The list of items in Table 47, if implemented, is itself part of a significant development of human resource strategies. The involvement of all employees and their unions will be a break-through for many hierarchically structured organisations where empowerment and involvement in decisions are not preferred options. Sharing the facts of the organisation will be too much for many. The idea of establishing two-way commu-nications with employees will be an advance for some organisations. Even the best organisations receive criticism from employees about the quality of communications during employee mapping surveys. Finally, while inevitability and momentum are key ways to build employee support, you must look for support – not acquiescence. The purpose is not to have sullen employees who believe nothing can be changed. Everything should be very much open to debate and change. Trust is crucial above all. People must believe that you will look after them. To breach trust is something that can be done only once, and the organisation pays for it long after the event. Benchmarking must not forget the employees.

Managing advances in benchmarking

If you are successful in the first stage of benchmarking you will probably be asked to move on to the bigger and more complex process problems. There are dangers, and these are identified in Table 48. You can create the feeling of momentum but you should not create the impression that all identified problems can be resolved quickly. Despite the early wins that you will correctly seek out if benchmarking is to succeed, you will certainly become embroiled in a long-term and even continual change programme. You may find that you need, or can achieve, incremental change of the type emerging from total quality programmes. Perhaps even more necessary is a require-ment for significant step changes that come about by dismantling much of the way some tasks are done, and rebuild-ing them in a new way. There are other possibilities that will emerge when benchmarking advances. It becomes inevitable at some stage that you must face the daunting complexity of the organisation. You may find that one department is under- or overresourced, either in people or physical resources, compared

Table 48

ADVANCED BENCHMARKING

- [ ] Remember, problems cannot be solved quickly.
- [ ] After some early wins, many problems will require the long haul.
- [ ] Remember that as you advance the complexities will grow.
- [ ] Consider modelling the organisation and its key processes.
- [ ] Map the various complexities.
- [ ] Guard against an immersion in metrics.
- [ ] Watch for symptoms of 'paralysis by analysis'.

with other organisations. In trying to make a change you then find that a particular activity that is done in a specific way is used by another department. Any changes you make to one department have an impact on the other. The consequence is that you have to change two departments, not one. Most organisations are so complex and interrelated that any change also has an impact somewhere else.

Some progress has been made on modelling key processes in this way (Ernst & Young and Andersen Consulting). A comprehensive metrics approach has been used and this will require appropriate IT support in many organisations because of the vastness of the numbers that emerge. The extraordinary complexity of the organisation means that the interrelationships become very difficult to grasp. In undertaking such an exercise you will need appropriate support, probably from a consultant or a specialist internal advice team. The effort required can be hard work and you will have to wait patiently for the really big achievements that the effort justifies. One word of caution is necessary – be on your guard that you are not analysing processes and decision areas more and more. You could be avoiding difficult decisions while seeming to address them. Paralysis by analysis is a common problem.

In searching for new ideas one organisation has carried out a 'brown paper exercise' with huge wall charts on which are mapped the organisation and its complex interrelations. Another company took over a room on the walls of which were hung scores of flip charts listing and mapping the complexities of the organisation. Look for these innovative ways of facing old problems.

The project plan

The most important aspect of project planning and control is to have a project plan (Bee and Bee 1997). This must be subject to regular review, update and change. An outline of a project management chart is given in Figure 11. It is essential that the project is managed and controlled in the rigorous and systematic way that this Figure implies. The time-scales are initially established, with those that have been achieved shown in solid lines, and those that are forecast in dotted lines, as shown in Figure 11. As time and the project progresses those items become clearer. The point is not to hold people to these time-scales but to manage according to them and understand why they change. So, for example, one result of benchmarking could be to widen performance management to cover all employees and to introduce the scorecard approach. In this case the development line plan could be extended to include such items as:

☐ Explain new processes to all employees.
☐ Define revised scorecard documentation.
☐ Train managers in handling the process.
☐ Phase implementation of performance.
☐ Establish links with payment procedures.

In this way the chart develops as the project grows.

In the end it is perhaps difficult to see the difference between what you have compared with any ordinarily derived project. Benchmarking has created the impetus for change by comparing internal performance with the identified best practices being carried on elsewhere. The change itself may look no different, but the source of it is.

Summary and conclusion

This chapter has covered the issues that arise in trying to implement benchmarking. In some ways it summarises many of the features of the preceding chapters. The important

Figure 11

A PROJECT MANAGEMENT CHART

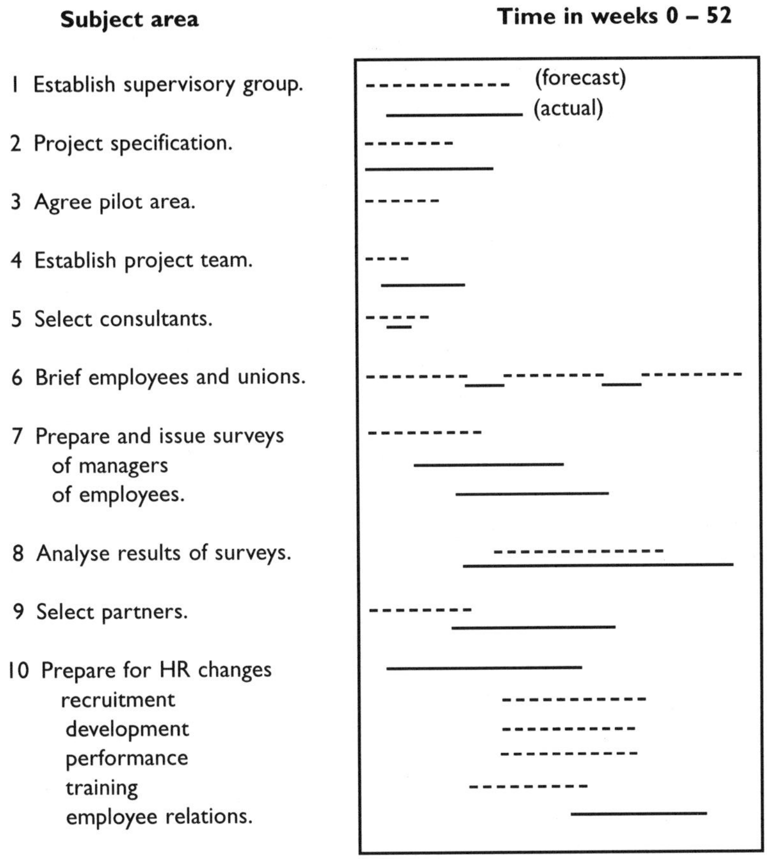

Subject area	Time in weeks 0 – 52

1 Establish supervisory group.	- - - - - - - - - - - (forecast) _____ (actual)
2 Project specification.	- - - - - - - _____
3 Agree pilot area.	- - - - - -
4 Establish project team.	- - - - ____
5 Select consultants.	- -_- -
6 Brief employees and unions.	- - - - - - - -__- - - - - - - -__- - - - - - - -
7 Prepare and issue surveys of managers of employees.	- - - - - - - - - _____ _____
8 Analyse results of surveys.	_____ - - - - - - - - - - - - - _____
9 Select partners.	- - - - - - - - _____
10 Prepare for HR changes recruitment development performance training employee relations.	_____ - _____

messages to get across are to select the pilot with care, to have a good project manager, build momentum and support, monitor progress carefully and, above all, remember your people and communicate with them.

12

USING CONSULTANTS

Why use consultants?

This chapter will look at the use of consultants. The questions you should ask yourself are the subject of this chapter. Whether you will employ consultant support depends to a large extent (but perhaps not exclusively) on the knowledge base that already exists within the organisation. If the organisation is large and has many areas of expertise within it why should you use consultants? There are a number of possible reasons why consultants are used in organisations. These can be analysed in turn so that you can decide whether they have relevance to your organisation, and how you will consider the points raised.

Providing an empathetic ear

The various reasons are listed in Table 49, the first of which is to have someone who will listen to you. It is easy to underestimate the need to have someone who can listen to problems – to have someone on whom to test ideas and who can suggest ways forward. Consultants can provide managers and leaders with emotional and intellectual support when things get tough. Usually this will be a senior consultant who is not involved in the day-to-day activity. This sort of assistance can be invaluable even if you do not employ major consulting support for a project. Of course, this may also affect the sort of company you will be looking for – if you decide you need consulting support at all. You can look at a major all-purpose consulting firm that will provide excellent analytical support and work with you throughout the project. It is also possible to find firms specialising in benchmarking and re-engineering processes. They may have a special IT benchmarking database that can be invaluable. Finally, you can consider the small consultancy which

Table 49

WHY USE CONSULTANTS?

- ☐ An empathetic ear.
- ☐ A fresh look at the organisation.
- ☐ Avoidance of political baggage.
- ☐ Provision of short-term resources.
- ☐ Knowledge of outside sources of supply.
- ☐ Expertise, expertise, expertise (and information).
- ☐ Help in finding benchmarking partners.

will perhaps be in a position to provide a less extensive service, but can still provide the support you may need.

Whatever expertise exists within the organisation, it can be useful at the start of something new to have a fresh view on your position. Someone from outside can often look at issues in a different way than you are used to.

Avoiding political baggage

While you might think that your organisation is capable of dealing with changes, there may still be a case for extra support. Many organisations find that so much time and effort has been invested in constructing the current process that it is beyond their capacity to consider significant changes to it. This will be the case particularly if the changes were hard fought for in the first place. The alliances that have been carefully constructed within the organisation may come tumbling down if the person who is part of them, or who even proposed them, was now to propose something different! This would be even more difficult where the review and change was being proposed by a person or department that had originally opposed the implementation of the structure or process. The advantage of consultants is that they should not be attached to a particular process in this way and should be free to tell the story as it is.

Providing short-term resources

It may be that the benchmarking exercise will swallow up resources, particularly in its early investigative and analytical phases. This problem can often be solved by employing consultants for a period. It is possible to contemplate a lead consultant or consultants who form a small core team. This can then be supported by a further team of dedicated professionals who undertake some major task (such as the preparation of an initial report) and then leave.

Of course, there are other ways of achieving dedicated short-term resources. Employees exist who go from job to job rather like internal consultants, but who spend a longer period 'employed' by one department. The advantage is that if you are lucky you may get a good group of people, but if you are looking for specialist knowledge support you may not be so lucky. At any event, whoever you look to provide the short-term resources and expertise, consultants are available and they can provide a useful (some companies would say essential) back-up service.

Knowledge of outside suppliers

In benchmarking terms it is necessary to consider how to get access to other companies and their data. This is where consultants have found a ready market. Benchmarking relies on having information available, sometimes from within the organisation, but usually from outside organisations that would not normally supply it to you freely.

Consultants will have links already established with the sources of supply of information. The consultants you choose may well have established self-help clubs. It is also important to recognise that many companies are not eager to become involved with every company that contacts them for assistance. The more well-known benchmarking companies quickly find that they become the target of countless queries and surveys. This is one reason for giving the analyses to consultants in the first place, as it takes the pressure off the organisation itself. You may have little to offer other organisations, particularly in the early stages. You will have little to offer until you have undertaken your initial analysis, surveys, and questionnaires and have highlighted your gap analysis. In these circumstances, using a consultant to gain access to the base data seems a sensible idea.

Expertise, expertise and expertise (and information)

It can be said that there are three important aspects that a consultant can add – expertise, expertise and expertise. This is probably the main reason that will motivate you to use consultants. They have been through it before. They will know what problems are likely to be encountered and have ideas to solve them. They know a lot about running project teams, about culture and changing it. They will have expertise in all these areas. Perhaps one word of caution is that some consulting groups may have less expertise in the HR area. If you are engaged purely in HR benchmarking, many consultants may be less appropriate. Some, such as Saratoga and Coopers & Lybrand have specialist HR people, but some hardly touch HR at all, preferring to concentrate on benchmarking the traditional areas of finance, production and quality control. However, most consultancies now recognise that the weakness of many change programmes (and benchmarking is a major change programme) is the failure to account for the human dimension. They are therefore building up the HR facilities and the HR expertise they are able to offer.

In addition to the access to information already mentioned, consultants have major expertise in other related benchmarking areas. An important aspect of the consultant's service is designing questionnaires to get at the information required quickly and efficiently. They can give advice on the type of question structure and the advantages of each; whether and where you should use multiple choice, forced choice, comparative scaled questions, and so on. They should also advise on undertaking the initial analysis with the organisation. It is particularly important to get this right as it may focus attention on a few assumed key activities in the future.

Table 50

HIRING A CONSULTANT

☐	Prepare a specification.
☐	Decide what you want.
☐	Ask for a presentation.
☐	Who will you work with?
☐	Who will they work with?
☐	Are they offering something new?
☐	Will they become part of the political baggage?

Hiring a consultant

If you decide to hire a consultant there are a number of points to consider, as shown in Table 50. It is essential that a specification of what you require is prepared. It is no good simply calling in consultants and ask them to prepare the specification for you. It will be sensible to regard the specification as a changeable document, but you must have a clear target so that the effect of any changes to the specification and their implications can be assessed.

The next step will be a preliminary informal exchange of views. This may be with a larger group of consultants from which you will shortlist two or three from which the final selection will be made. This presentation is very important and will demonstrate the knowledge they have of the area of work and how much they have understood the needs of the organisation. At this stage you should expect to receive a proposal, such as in Table 51. It has to be realistic in terms of time and money. Does the internal project organisation seem reasonable to the consultant, and what suggestions might be made for adaptations? If the consultant's own computer services are to be used then you will need to ensure compatibility with your own systems. This will be particularly important if large data transfers become likely, with all the attendant problems of inputting errors and the time and cost involved if manual input is necessary. You should look at the draft project chart (discussed in the last chapter) to see how the project is progressing. An assessment can then be made as to whether

Table 51

CONSULTANT'S PROPOSAL:

WHAT ARE YOU LOOKING FOR?

Introduction
- ☐ What do they know about benchmarking?
- ☐ What do they know about your problem?
- ☐ What management steering is proposed by them to you?

Project purpose
- ☐ Is this clearly set out?
- ☐ Is it clear how you can stop Topsy?
- ☐ Is it clear what you will achieve?

Project benefits
- ☐ Have these been worked on?
- ☐ Do they make sense?
- ☐ Are they novel, creative or routine?

Project schedule
- ☐ Are specific steps listed?
- ☐ Have they commented on your draft?
- ☐ Are changes to your ideas explained?
- ☐ Has time been allowed for building support, training, etc?

Progress reports
- ☐ Are there milestones of achievement?
- ☐ Will there be tight project control?
- ☐ Can you retain control?

People
- ☐ How well qualified are the individual consultants?
- ☐ Is it clear who you will work with?
- ☐ Will there be any subcontracting?
- ☐ Will people provided be credible?
- ☐ Are there facilities to use your own people?

the technical, financial and human resources are likely to be sufficient.

One important consideration is the person with whom you will work. It is highly probable that a senior executive from the consultancy will make the sales pitch. You should insist on having at least part of the presentation given by whoever would handle your account. Do not be misled by a senior consultant who says that he will handle the account. Senior executives in consultancies are busy people and they are simply not available on a day-to-day basis. You should ask the consultancy who will be in strategic charge of the project and who will be your day-to-day contact. Of course, the other side of the coin is that you should have present the person who will be in day-to-day charge of the project. If the project leader has been appointed then that person should be present (and should also do a large part of the talking).

Pricing the job

It is important to be clear about how the job will be priced. Major consultancies tend to price on a per-day basis and they are reluctant to give reductions, even for larger jobs. One way round the problem is to identify the task and ask for an all-in price for it, if the consultant is willing. You must, however, be realistic. Consultants are in business to make money. Individual consultants have 'sales' targets to meet. The nature of the relationship, and who owns the information that comes from it, are very important questions to be clear about. Consultants will, however, always respect the confidences of a client and there is no need to be concerned on that account.

You can hire consultants for about £600 per day, but £1000 to £2000 per day is more usual for experts in a field. You can see how quickly the charges will mount. You must insist on regular interim billing. The telephone call, followed by a discussion that you had last week has cost the consultant time, and therefore money – do not be surprised if you are billed for it. Finally, you need to be clear about expenses and how they will be billed. Unfortunately, if they are not capped in some way there is little motivation to prevent costs escalating.

Questioning the consultant's data

A further consideration is what expertise, in terms of general information and hard data, is being offered. It has been suggested that some consultancies have relabelled old techniques as benchmarking and process re-engineering and are marketing them accordingly. There is nothing wrong with that approach as long as it is clear to all involved. There are, after all, many similarities between various management techniques.

Finally, you need to reflect on how the consultant will avoid becoming part of the political baggage that was discussed at the start of this chapter. One of the main purposes of a consultant is to provide a 'helicopter' view of your organisation. The consultant must be able to provide a second opinion without feeling ownership of any of the problems or issues that, by inference, are being criticised. Yet understanding problems and getting close to you is the consultant's job. There is a paradox here whereby all consultant relationships are essentially limited in time. You must review this matter to test continually whether you are still getting the same fresh approach from your consultant that you did at the beginning. Finally, the progress of the project and the work of the consultant should be measured against some sort of time and activity chart of the type discussed in the last chapter. It should list all the various stages, such as the investigation phase, how long it will take to prepare questionnaires, and when they will be issued. Timescales for selecting partners, deciding benchmarks, and how you will build support, should all be set out. For each item, make clear when it will take place and how much time the consultant will spend. The extent to which timescales are met and the reasons for falling behind target can be discussed at regular review and milestone meetings.

Summary and conclusion

Consultants have their place, especially to support major new initiatives and to undertake the peaks of work that result. You must also make use of the skills within your own organisation while being aware of the expertise and knowledge base that a consultant will have. We have discussed the empathetic ear that a consultant provides and how useful they are in providing short-term resources. You must have a clear specification and know what the costs will be. However, remember that benchmarking is about making comparisons both internally and externally. You must recognise that internally you are less likely to have someone who can ask with the innocence of the child 'why are we doing it that way?', or 'why do we do it at all?' The consultant is well suited to asking questions about the emperor's mode of dress!

13

WHY BENCHMARKING FAILS – AVOIDING PROBLEMS

Missing out the people

This chapter looks at the reasons why a benchmarking project sometimes fails.

We have already learnt that if benchmarking is going to lead anywhere, and is not going to stop simply at statistical or metric comparison, we are at some stage going to become involved in changing and reorganising work. We know that you cannot sort out structural or cost problems, or excess manpower, or having too few people of the right skill, and so on, without looking behind the problem at how tasks are actually done. If you do not account for people's views in such change, or if you do not have their support, then you are risking failure. People and their unions can make change difficult to carry through and it can be tempting, but wrong, to ignore them altogether. Even harmful redundancy programmes can be introduced – as many companies have done – with a degree of sensitivity if it is carefully planned.

Would it have been possible to fashion modern industries out of the UK privatisations, without tens of thousands of redundancies? When people talk of 'integrating people and business policies to create a coherent framework' does it mean anything, or is it just 'management speak'? Given the things that had to be done, perhaps people could not find another solution. The point here is that the choice can be made as to the manner in which changes are achieved. In many privatisations people were given time to reflect on their own position. Individually, people had an element of choice. In one organisation a benchmarking study of redundancy terms, and related reward and conditions issues, established the benchmark of what needed to be paid. So even in difficult times the employee's interests can still be listened to. Not to do so would be to fail.

There are examples of organisations that have changed systems or procedures, or cut costs through delayering, without thinking through the people implications. What of training? What of career structure? What of pay and equal value? What of all such questions that need looking at? To ignore them would be to tempt failure. You need the support of employees, trade unions and managers. Ignore any of these groups and the project is at risk.

Unrealistic expectations

One of the key areas where benchmarking can fail is if the organisation has unrealistic expectations of what it will achieve. The unrealistic expectations can come from a misunderstanding of the technique. It is true that some definitions of benchmarking suggest great possibilities for change and development, but there is no magic involved. It is also possible that the 'hype' that comes with any new process or technique has led to overselling. Most organisations, however, while they may be shooting at the highest level of change, are realistic enough to know what solid performance will achieve. Failure even to achieve at this modest level can be a result of unrealistic expectations

A failure to understand culture

One area where benchmarking can fail is because there is insufficient understanding of the cultural implications of change. It is not sufficient to work on a change programme if the organisation does not have the infrastructure to carry it through. It is possible that the changes proposed are more than employees could handle. There is no point proposing to change command and control structures significantly by, say, removing management levels unless the managers who remain, or the people they are in charge of, understand the implications. It is not feasible to 'de-layer'(to use the jargon) and then expect managers to have knowledge of every small detail, as they had in the past. They will just not have the time available.

It is not feasible to develop systems and processes that depend on commitment, openness, mutual support and teamwork if the traditional way in which business is approached is by blame, deference and holding back. It is essential that such aspects are considered before the most significant changes are implemented. New processes that demand new ways of working cannot be implemented on existing cultures; it will not work.

Recognising the time and cost of learning

For these reasons, organisations that are trying to implement major change must allocate time for employees to learn of any new vision or values that the changes imply. It is not uncommon for all employees in an organisation to be put through a learning experience when the organisation is trying to change the direction that the organisation is taking. Such changes are not cheap; resources must be allocated. To try to change corporate direction without setting time aside to explain to employees the reasons and implications is a recipe for certain failure.

This is why the mapping exercise described in Chapter 3 is so important. An exercise that finds out what people think about change will identify the likely problems that the organisation may encounter. Here there is a significant cost. If the organisation cannot, or will not, pay the cost involved it is far better to lower expectations. It is not ethical to attempt to introduce a programme without proper preparation, and employees will repay you with their cynicism.

There is another aspect that comes before that of employees learning about culture or new occupations. People need training in benchmarking to believe in the process. It is essential that people talk about the programme and its intention. You must get them talking to other organisations, or to their peers who have tried it in your own organisation. Get them to do anything that helps them internalise and understand the possibilities of benchmarking. Without this emphasis on training in benchmarking, or in change processes and procedures, failure will be a possibility and expectations are unlikely to be met.

A failure to implement benchmarking strategically

Another problem will result if changes are made to one aspect of the business without proper preparation elsewhere. If, for example, a business decides, after a benchmarking exercise, to decentralise HR activity to line managers, chaos can result if the ground is not properly prepared. Managers who are now free from HR constraints can recruit whom they wish, pay what they want, train when they want to, develop employees if they feel like it, and so on. The consequences have been seen in many situations. One engineering company recognised that comparisons showed that other organisations' costs were achieved by decentralised HR. They introduced such a change and eventually fell foul of industrial tribunals, equal opportunities legislation and safety problems from having inadequately prepared managers handling such issues. Such changes must be introduced with care if matters are not to deteriorate. It also must be remembered that someone still has to be responsible for setting the HR standards that the organisation finds acceptable.

What the previous example highlighted was the failure that results from implementing only one part of a strategy – if indeed a strategy exists at all. If the organisation believes that it is possible to implement change on a piecemeal basis it is almost bound to fail. The bigger and more significant the change the more likely is failure. This is simply because change affects not just the area being looked at, but all the others who use the process in any way. For example, one company removed the forms used at interviews because their benchmarking showed they were overloaded with bureaucracy. The result was that another unit could no longer meet the needs for equal opportunity monitoring and were severely criticised at an Industrial Tribunal. This is a small example, but the decentralising of HR to line managers can be a problem if not properly thought through. What is required is an agreed policy on pay and reward, recruitment, training, equal opportunities, employment rights, and so on. The line departments, having agreed the policies, need to be trained in their application.

Desire for a quick fix

One failing that underlies much of the foregoing is a desire for a 'quick fix'. This is something that is a particular problem for HR. Managers seem to believe that HR is something that can be analysed quickly (whereas their new audit procedures must be lovingly nurtured and introduced with the greatest of care!). Any instant decision is almost bound to fail. Any response to benchmarking that results in cutting out large numbers of employees may be a quick fix too far. Many organisations have sacked employees, to find only subsequently that mistakes have been made and recruitment is then required. A quick look at the HR statistics, followed by a site visit to a company doing well with its HR policies, cannot be immediately transferred to your own environment.

Expecting too much from the metrics

Measurement (or metrics) is one of the most attractive aspects of benchmarking to many managers. This point is made forcefully by those involved in benchmarking. Metrics have their strengths because you get 'real live data' that facilitate comparison. But there is also a risk of failure. The very ease of comparison creates a trap that many organisations have fallen into.

The reason this can lead to failure is that what is right for one organisation is not necessarily right for another. Any organisation that is operating in one type of industry is in a quite different situation from one operating in another. HR policies that work perfectly well in one organisation may be unacceptable in another where the political spotlight may make an innovation unacceptable. For example, some organisations happily reward employees with overseas holidays and breaks for excellent achievement. Imagine the outcry if this reward process was applied to a school or a hospital trust!

It is essential that care is taken to ensure that the organisation with which comparisons are being made is operating in a similar environment. Where it is not, you must understand the implications of the differences. Context is all important. Is your company in service or manufacturing, building power stations or marketing and design?; in a market that is expanding or contracting? All these affect the relevance of the numbers. It is crucial that while investigating the numbers you never lose sight of the practices – how, what and why you do things, is critical.

Leadership and project management

Above all, projects fail when they are badly managed and unclearly set out. The project manager is crucial. He or she must be someone who knows what project management is; that much should be taken for granted. Above all, however, the benchmarking exercise should be entrusted to a project manager who is also the process owner. If you have two or three exercises taking place simultaneously, then put process owners in charge of each project. It will not work if you have a support function in charge. No one will feel responsible, or fight the corner when problems emerge. If the project is badly led the project team cannot function. If the 'board' or other group in charge does not lead and support then the project benchmarking will fail. Indeed, this is one way that managers can sabotage projects. They feel a need to go along with the project but have no sympathy with it, so they make sure that the leader is ineffective.

You can usually discover the real support for a project by looking at the person in charge. As a consultant will tell you, the insider whom he or she gets to deal with tells them about the real status of benchmarking. What arrangements have been made for employee briefing and feedback? What resource allocation has been made for systems changes and IT costs? All of these, and other aspects, give clues as to what the organisation really thinks about benchmarking. If leadership is inadequate then benchmarking will fail. It is far better to recognise such problems early on and either get out or lower your sights to an activity where leadership and support are forthcoming.

NIH: Not invented here

Perhaps the main reason for failure is the rejection of ideas for change coming from outside the organisation – 'not invented here'. Benchmarking depends on a willingness to look at other organisations intelligently, and to learn from them. At its simplest, benchmarking consists of comparing with other organisations and then establishing the benchmark of achievement, reviewing the processes involved and working out how to move towards the benchmark at a strategic level. If your organisation is obsessed with 'territory' and 'turf wars', if there is an obsession with pride as to what has been done in the past, you will not be able to make use of benchmarking.

Of course, all statistics can misrepresent the real situation. Of course, all analyses and tables and charts are summations. Any table does not tell the whole story. The question is, are you willing to learn what might be learnt? The issue of 'not invented here' will be recognised by many managers. In its good aspects it is, of course, a reflection of natural pride. But can people get beyond that? There is a natural resistance to change, especially change that impacts close to home. This is known as 'proxiphobia' – the fear of being in proximity. It is why an executive bravely reorganises, and pushes items against vigorous trade union opposition, and yet fails utterly to deal with the overstaffing in his own HQ section. The nearer something is to you, or to something you care about, the more proxiphobia and the NIH syndrome take effect. This item is so important, some organisations so closed to change – that major culture change initiatives have been directed at changing it (Childress and Senn 1995). Unless this area is considered, above all others, benchmarking will not so much fail as not get started! The evidence is apparent in the reaction to league tables in hospitals and schools. Almost universal rejection is heaped upon them. There is, however, a lesson here. The more exposed a manager feels, and the more he or she is attacked, the less inclined is he or she to change. The NIH syndrome can be lessened by showing managers the information privately and asking for the areas to be reviewed. In this way the barriers can start to fall. If the deliverer of the statistics is looking for public humiliation he or she should not be surprised when people rush to explain and defend themselves.

Collecting and analysing data

A common failing in benchmarking is to allocate insufficient resources to collecting data in the first place. It takes time to establish realistic partners who have an interest in benchmarking. There is no point beginning if the comparator organisation has no similar activities, and trying to get data out of an unwilling partner is very hard indeed.

You must think through what you are going to benchmark and what you expect it to deliver. You must know when you are going to stop collecting data and start to do something with it. All the time you must remind yourself that the metrics will be only part of the story. You must make sure that you recognise that time will have to be spent collecting data, but also that you know when to stop to prevent 'paralysis by analysis'.

A start can be made by joining clubs and organisations that can make other organisations' data available – but even then, data collection is not simple. Competitive benchmarking is particularly difficult because of the time it takes to establish the trust involved.

Badly prepared project specification

One area where difficulty can be encountered is in the project specification. If you are not clear what is intended, or other managers believe that the target is some other issue, then failure can result for some – even though others may consider the exercise a success. This point is particularly important if you intend to employ consultants. You must set out comprehensively the specification and tasks expected, together with strictly allocated costs and time-scales. The disappointment that can be experienced with consultants is usually caused by an initially unclear specification. You must be clear at the beginning what the project is intended to achieve, how it will be managed and therefore what role you expect for the consultants. This area of project management is so important that if you are at all unsure how to go about it you should undertake training in it. You could do worse than read the recently published IPD text on project management (Bee and Bee 1997).

Summary and conclusion

These are some key reasons for failure at benchmarking. They are summarised for convenience in Table 52. Foremost among the reasons for failure are: giving insufficient concern to people issues, not dealing with NIH, inadequate training and spending too long on analysis. For many, benchmarking is likely to be a new activity. Even if some part of the organisation has some experience of it, there will be many departments that have had little or no exposure. The opportunity exists to use comparison of numbers and then processes with other organisations to establish priorities for change and progress. A benchmarking project can survive if one or two of the items discussed in this chapter are poorly delivered or neglected all together. But the more that are deficient, the greater the risk of failure is. Perhaps the most useful advice is a plea to keep it simple and avoid overcomplexity. It is better to achieve 80 per cent of something quickly than to go for 100 per cent and risk total failure.

Table 52

WHY BENCHMARKING FAILS

☐	You have unrealistic expectations.
☐	Failure to address culture.
☐	Failure to allow for the time and cost of training.
☐	Failure to develop a strategy.
☐	Desire for a 'quick fix'.
☐	Focusing on Metrics – forgetting How? What? Why?
☐	No proper leadership.
☐	NIH – 'not invented here' – becomes an issue.
☐	Collecting and analysing data.
☐	Badly prepared project specification.

14

BUSINESS PROCESS RE-ENGINEERING

Looking at business process re-engineering (BPR)

This chapter looks at business process re-engineering (BPR). Why does a book on benchmarking include a chapter on BPR? There are two reasons. First, BPR is closely related to benchmarking. When you seek to implement benchmarking you will inevitably run into BPR. The second reason is that BPR has been sold with such 'hype'. It has also been so heavily criticised that much of that criticism is in danger of spilling over on to benchmarking. Reviewing the publicity that surrounds BPR you may be forgiven for concluding that the prospect of unrestrained growth and improvement in efficiency lies before you – it is only necessary to grasp the opportunity provided by this latest corporate panacea dealing with the radical reordering of how work in business is done.

People are deeply suspicious of 'panaceas'; we have been here before. Table 53 lists some of those that have waxed and waned over the years. Fewer people now believe that you can ascertain the length of time it takes to complete a task by breaking the task into its component parts. Books were published making pages and pages of detailed analyses available to time and motion engineers. It is perhaps easy to forget how this sort of analysis was the foundation of bonus schemes and work-studied incentive payment schemes that determined how huge numbers of people in industry were paid. They still exist in some form in some industries, although they are now less fashionable, and in general 'time and motion studies' have had their day.

During the 1960s and 1970s planning was all the rage. Managers were enticed to remove uncertainty by forecasting.

Table 53

PANACEAS OF THE PAST AND THE PRESENT

Yesterday's answers:
- ☐ Time and motion.
- ☐ Management by objectives.
- ☐ Theory X and theory Y.
- ☐ Blake's managerial grid.
- ☐ Corporate and long-range planning.
- ☐ Quality circles.

Today's answers:
- ☐ Just-in-time production.
- ☐ Total quality management.
- ☐ Radicalism – 'In Search of Excellence'.

The argument was that if we knew a little more about the uncertainties that existed we could improve the quality of decision-making significantly. So complex models, and even more complex internal planning procedures, were fashioned to handle this new wonder process. Corporate planning had arrived. People are now much more realistic about planning. No one tries to foretell the future, and we find it difficult to comprehend that there was once a world where there was such certainty that people believed that you could.

To different degrees this is true of all the ideas listed in Table 53, the 'panaceas of the past'. Who now proposes Blake's grid for their managers, or talks of MBO (Management by Objectives)? Perhaps quality circles have now been overtaken by total quality, and that in turn by TQM. Are there not signs that the proponents of those techniques are busy reinventing themselves to maintain their relevance?

Perhaps no one now proposes sending the entire organisation on Blake's grid, and many lessons have been learned, but many modern approaches have a not unfamiliar resonance. For example, the potential conflict between the business interest and the people interest is fundamental to criticisms of much of the management activity identified by the confident 'new right'. Yet this conflict between people and production, and the attempt to resolve it, was at the heart of Blake's management grid. Is this not a new version of an old idea?

Blake, in his grid, talks of 9–1 production-oriented managers who ignored people, and 1–9 people-oriented managers who worked on relationships but ignored business needs. It is interesting to look at the British Quality Foundation's model of business excellence with its 'people' and 'business results' axes, or the components of the 'balanced scorecard' approach to management performance, to see how these items progress and develop. Perhaps what we are doing now owes more to the past than some presenters would have us understand.

BPR and benchmarking

For the purpose of this book it is necessary to sort out the differences between BPR and benchmarking before it is possible to look at the criticisms of 'panacea' and 'hype' that have been targeted at BPR. Benchmarking is concerned with establishing a standard of performance by internal and external measurement and then comparing that standard with other standards derived from elsewhere. Re-engineering, on the other hand, is about the radical internal change of processes. They are closer than might be imagined from a cursory look at such descriptions.

In benchmarking it is necessary to discuss and question another unit or organisation in a rigorous and systematic way. How is the work organised? Do they interview fewer candidates? Are their present procedures tougher? Do they give in-depth feedback? It should be obvious that in undertaking benchmarking in this way you are now scrutinising core HR and business processes. You are looking critically at where you spend resources and highlighting possible ways of improvement. This is exactly what you would be doing in BPR. So are the activities different?

What are the differences?

What are the differences between benchmarking and BPR? It has already been shown that both can have the same result – a major restructuring of how processes are undertaken. Clearly, benchmarking could not just stop at the first cursory level of comparison, investigation and analysis. In the BPR view 'process management' is fundamentally different. All departments become organised not on functional or departmental grounds but are built around core business processes. This can be the result of benchmarking, but the key difference is that BPR proclaims it as an essential feature while in benchmarking it may be only a useful result. BPR has been heavily 'sold' in a particular way. It has set out a challenge to managers to sweep away old processes and change completely how the organisation undertakes its tasks. Benchmarking is not defined in this extreme way and has more cautious (some would say safer and realistic, others would cringingly say less ambitious) aims.

The 'hype' of BPR

It is interesting to see the enthusiasm with which proponents of BPR can adopt in their presentations. Michael Hammer, Tom Davenport and James Champy have become the leaders of BPR, with immodest book titles such as 'The Re-engineering Revolution' and 'Re-engineering the Corporation – a manifesto for business revolution'. In comparison, Tom Davenport's excellent text entitled 'Process Innovation' seems tame! These books have sold millions of copies and appeared in high-street bookshop windows and best sellers' lists. Was everyone 'conned'?

What is offered is a way to improve efficiency by getting rid of old 'dead wood' in the enterprise. This offers the prospect of improving services or profit levels, all at reduced cost. You have only to be brave enough to challenge the *status quo* and, like Jericho's fabled walls, resistance will crumble in the face of the rigorous onslaught of the righteous. Managers who attend lectures given by such presenters could be forgiven for thinking that they were attending a religious revivalist meeting – such is the fervour, enthusiasm and humour with which the message is presented. Sometimes the line between the medium and the message becomes blurred, or even obscured, and it is possible to end up feeling entertained rather than educated.

What is the BPR message?

It is interesting to look at what is said in favour of BPR by such writers and presenters. The first point is that it starts out 'radically' to redesign business processes to bring about 'dramatic' improvements in performance. Apart from the use of two such words, 'radically' and 'dramatic', along with the intention of 'starting over' or ' starting from scratch', there is also the use of the key words of the concept, namely the 'redesigning' of business 'processes'. These would be widely accepted as necessary, but they are not new. Many of the former proponents of the management initiatives listed in Table 53 would be satisfied with a definition of those tasks in terms of 'redesigning business processes'. There is more continuity over time in these ideas than might be supposed.

The context of BPR

It is context that matters. The BPR analysis is driven by a modern business context where change is taking place at an extraordinary pace. Technology help to provide a response to the change, but it also makes that change necessary as some companies use IT more efficiently and successfully to advance their products and services. The bankruptcy files of receivers are replete with failed companies who did not respond to the needs of the twentieth and twenty-first centuries by changing their processes. They continued to manufacture products that people did not want, or to provide processes that customers would not pay for. Whether it is cars, ships, banks, football teams, computers, handmade shirts, factories making white sliced bread, schools or hospitals, everyone is having to change their processes; those that do not will sink without trace.

Successful BPR?

One of the larger telephone service providers in the United States re-engineered its customer contact services. The previous arrangements for repairing a telephone consisted of the routines listed in Table 54. The procedure was a bureaucracy full of hand-ons or pass-overs to the next person in the chain.

Table 54

CUSTOMER CONTACT AT AN INSURANCE COMPANY

Old	Re-engineered
☐ Customer contact.	☐ Customer contact.
☐ Repair check, take details.	☐ Repair advocate completes job and
☐ Line-tester tests line.	tests line:
☐ Office technician called.	– software modified
☐ Office makes appointment.	– problem located
☐ Technician repairs phone.	– appointment arranged
	– customer visited.

There are many opportunities for error in communication leading to referrals (or hand-offs). All this was taking place, of course, while the customer was waiting with a telephone that did not work! The result was a poor customer satisfaction rating of under 1 per cent. Having undertaken benchmarking with other major companies, the company found where the problem lay. Their customer contact and repair procedure did not match the competition. The process was full of delays caused by hand-offs, pass-ons and controls. They set about 're-engineering' the process – that is, totally redesigning it.

The new re-engineered process has resulted in one-stop shop 'repair advocates' who are able to achieve a resolution of customer problems in over 40 per cent of cases, as shown in Table 54, while the customer is still on the telephone. The implications of such a change for customer satisfaction and reduced maintenance costs are huge. This example also shows the close links between different initiatives, in this case between benchmarking and re-engineering. Sometimes the change will reorganise tasks into single jobs. In the example this resulted in renaming the job as a 'repair advocate' (Hammer and Champy 1994). It is easy to dismiss such changes, but they are a visible statement to the outside world that things have changed. It is one of this author's regrets that he prevented a manager changing the jobs of 'clerks' to 'customer representatives' for fear of union reaction and the grading claims that would have resulted. It is, however, just as likely that knowledge barriers would prevent change, and so an alternative approach would be to group jobs into teams where people can work easily together. It is also possible for people to improve their knowledge gradually so that phase two removes differentiation entirely, and one person does most of the tasks.

The idea of teamworking is important because it allows highly skilled people to retain the separation that knowledge brings, while reducing the inevitable pass-overs and hand-offs that occur when teams are artificially separated. This is very important. As has been suggested, organisations tend to be structured to meet internal needs. They reflect the power structure of functions and professionalisms. This is the same whether you are dealing with schools, hospitals, major utilities or manufacturing. The company is organised to deliver its product or service in ways which meet its internal needs, not the needs of customers. It is hardly surprising that managers will make the political trade-offs that are necessary to make progress, but it must be recognised that a price is being paid by a loss of focus on the customer's needs. This, then, is the BPR message – a radical redesign of processes to effect dramatic improvements in service or product quality, which is provided to meet the business needs. It is important that those needs are defined by customers who pay for the product or service on the open market, not by self-serving bureaucrats.

What is necessary for BPR?

Having considered what BPR is about, what do its adherents say is necessary for success? Some ideas drawn from the literature (Bramham 1996) (but not specifically in these terms) are given in Table 55. Many of them will probably strike the reader as areas that are being considered within their own organisation. Let us examine the list given in that table.

It will be obvious that top management support is necessary for any major initiative. A project leader is also essential, as is clear knowledge of what it is that is being reviewed. Perhaps not so obvious is that any major change project should be led by a 'process owner'. This means a line manager who is part of the department being changed. There exist too many opportunities for responsibility to become diffused when

Table 55

WHAT BPR NEEDS TO SUCCEED

- ☐ Top management leadership.
- ☐ A re-engineering project leader.
- ☐ Detailed understanding of the work done.
- ☐ Process-led change.
- ☐ Getting rid of NIH syndrome.
- ☐ Being clear what the business is for.
- ☐ Being clear about values and culture.
- ☐ Measure and count again and again.
- ☐ Coaches, not managers.
- ☐ Replacement of corporate discipline with corporate spirit.
- ☐ An end to adversarial strategies.
- ☐ Introduction of growth, support and teamwork.
- ☐ An ending to functional power.
- ☐ Getting rid of command and control.

accountability rests with a 'change unit' or with the 'corporate planner', or 'productivity department', and so on. Such people are unlikely to have the necessary knowledge – but even if they have that knowledge, what they lack is the vital ingredient of accountability for results.

The concept of 'not invented here' is a fundamental problem in process re-engineering. It is equally relevant to many other ideas and change projects, and it is especially crucial to benchmarking. This is because benchmarking starts with an assumption that it is a good thing to be able to compare yourself with other organisations. The second assumption is that something useful can be learned from the results. If you cannot overcome internal resistance caused by NIH it will not be possible to make much progress. It is said that this is an essential prerequisite to BPR, but it is also the bedrock of benchmarking. An understanding of culture and the extent to which existing organisation value systems militate against change is crucial to any initiative that threatens the *status quo*. Looking at the other items listed, the need to base decisions on fact has long been pressed on managers. The need for coaching and support has been around for years, along with the idea of teamwork as an approach to lessen the destructive aspects of individualism and any general adversarial way of working.

Finally, there is the desire to break functional power and command and control ways of working. There is nothing new in this. Tom Peters (Peters and and Waterman 1982) was arguing in the late 1970s and early 1980s for breaking functional control over employees who wanted to serve customers. No one really suggested that all functionalism was bad and that command and control was wholly inappropriate. We all knew that you could not run a police service or the armed forces or the emergency services without command and control. Although perhaps less so, the same point is also true when considering a company. Both command and control clearly have important roles to play.

A problem of culture?

If it is possible to support a list such as that given in Table 55, why have there been such heavy criticisms of process re-engineering? Are the criticisms ill-founded? Perhaps a clue can be found in the language used in the way it is said, that BPR will be achieved. BPR is presented almost as a battle between good and evil. Instead of cautiously moving to a modified agenda, the talk is all about 'sweeping away' and 'starting over'. Perhaps this radicalism is the key to the problem.

It is, perhaps, sensible to recognise that the language and the source of the ideas are sufficient to irritate many academics and thinkers in the UK and Europe. Much of the BPR material emanates from US consultants and this can be a problem. Re-engineering is sold (like all products in the US!) with a vigour and enthusiasm which, in the UK at least, is perhaps seen as inappropriate. Terms like 're-engineering revolution', and 'the ordeal of management' are too lurid for many Anglo-Europeans. Even terms such as 'downsizing' are taken as insults, as the user of such terms tries to soften and perhaps conceal the true intention behind the actions being taken. Book titles such as the 'Maverick' or 'Re-engineering the Corporation – a manifesto for business revolution' will irritate some people, although they will also make friends. To attend a conference led by Michael Hammer is to be treated to a *tour de force* of insights and sharp criticism of what is wrong, presented in a very funny and enthusiastic style. It is perhaps true that many people who attend such sessions remember the jokes more than the content, but they are usually lifted and inspired and always have a good time. In all this there is, perhaps, a cultural separation between what the US and UK/Europe feel is the correct way to approach education in a business technique.

But that cannot be the whole story. We have been used to a succession of North American academic consultants putting forward their ideas. We have listened to them all, and many have found a ready UK/European audience. When Tom Peters in 1984 tried to persuade us to blow up the executive dining room, or sack all the executives, or paint out the executive parking places, or let an employee stop the production line we did not take him literally. We understood the message. Why has this not worked for re-engineering?

Criticism of BPR

'There is a new-look menu over at the Consultants Cafe. Good old soup du TQM and change management pâté are off. Perhaps you would care to try some business process re-engineering instead? '

In this way Hugh Willmott makes his position clear in respect of BPR with this quotation (Willmott 1994). Somewhat later the IPD journal *People Management* wrote the obituary for BPR in its May 1996 issue (Mumford and Hendricks 1996). What criticism lay behind those attacks? A key point is the potential that BPR has for destroying work as we currently know it. The BPR emphasis on information technology is not concerned with delivering existing manufacturing products and services electronically, but with the total transformation of those processes. In itself there can be nothing wrong with using computers in this way. We know that increasing sophistication and speed of access provided by computers now make possible processes that could not exist before. We know that huge areas of management and the professions are under threat from the advance of expert systems. An example would be pensions and payroll departments. Those decisions are gradually being seen for what they are – which is complex decision trees of rule processes that computers are in a much better position to handle more consistently, and indeed more accurately. Now there are just the areas of human judgement left. This is fine for those highly educated people who can do the work, and who can get access to it. It is not so fine for the people who are made redundant. It is perhaps in the manner of those changes that doubts begin to emerge. BPR promises radical improvements in business processes covering product development, quality, service and delivery times. The key word is 'radical' – not 'gradual' or 'incremental'. The emphasis is on 'starting over' and not embedding the sterility and outdated past within 21st century silicon! This is the language of BPR. There is no room here for the incremental change that was behind TQM. We are obliged by BPR to question all our conventional assumptions. What has become of the people? Can you really take a selection of tasks and then simply compress them into one?

There is nothing new in this questioning of the usefulness of a rigid bureaucracy. The idea of an organic, matrix-type structure surfaced in the 1960s (see eg Burns and Stalker 1961). The problem comes with the radical idea that 'goal displacement and organisational politics' can simply be brushed aside by a vigorous leader and the use of IT systems.

Downsizing

There is one area more than any other that highlights the general doubts that many people have about BPR, and this relates to employees. Although Hammer says that BPR is not about reducing the numbers of people employed, this can be an inevitable result as processes are streamlined and simplified. Will that not create considerable strains within the organisation? At what point does getting rid of 'dead wood' become getting rid of potentially productive workers? What sense is there in cutting out apprentice training and employee development – both done in the name of re-engineering to make efficiency savings? (See Bramham 1994.)

How are all these re-engineered processes to be carried out –
by employees, of course! Are employees 'infinitely malleable'
and capable of undertaking the extraordinary new ranges of
work that will be imposed upon them? Those who survive
must work longer hours and, despite the slogans to the
contrary, often feel they work 'harder' rather than just
'smarter'. For this fortunate group, there is the prospect of
career advancement, or at least a career and, detractors would
say, eventual 'burnout' and personal premature exit deals! This
has all been argued elsewhere with some force:
'For the mass whose jobs have been re-engineered out of
these companies, there is the increasingly restricted prospect of
occupying the lowly paid, temporary jobs that service tomorrow's 'networks', 'information brokers' ... (Willmott 1994).
This is the Achilles' heel of BPR. Employees are implicitly
assumed by BPR to be infinitely malleable. Any antagonism to
BPR is interpreted as *inertia*, rather than warrantable resistance to change, which can be dissolved by the persuasive
powers of senior management. HRM specialists, in particular,
may question whether the ambitions of BPR are consistent
with the distinctive qualities of 'human resources'. The same
article continues '... from this perspective, it is not BPR's
inflated sense of novelty so much as its shallow, technicist
appreciation of the human dimension of organisational change
that renders it vulnerable to failure and must be answered, not
least by HRM specialists' (Willmott 1994).

This is a severe criticism. The message given by BPR seems
to suggest that the human dimension is somehow a problem
to be sidelined and dealt with by a sweet talking HR specialist.
BPR's supporters would perhaps deny this and respond that it
was simply badly applied BPR. There are ethical considerations
about how a job is done that need to be carefully considered
and fully understood. There are important sociological,
psychological and political considerations that accompany any
change, but more especially change of such a dramatic nature
as that proposed by BPR.

The problem presumably is that the pace of change in business generally has led managers to wonder whether they can
afford to wait. The *People Management* article stressed the
value of an alternative 'socio-technical school' approach which

has been around for many years. It incorporates a concern for people rather than simply axing jobs. It argues for a recognition of a need to preserve the quality of working life.

Change in haste, regret at leisure

Many organisations engaged in BPR have found that while dramatic results were achieved in changing individual processes there was an overall decline in performance. Eugene Hall voiced some of these doubts in the *McKinsey Quarterly* published in 1994. The problem seemed to be a failure to understand how the organisation and its processes worked and hung together. If one or two major variables were changed then a process may indeed be speeded up, but what of the effects on the rest of the organisation?

This is typical of what happened at a US insurance company. This company changed its way of dealing with customers so that some 80–90 per cent of enquiries and sales could be handled on the spot with only exceptions being passed to specialists in legal and accounting. The improvements in processing efficiency were phenomenal. The achievement is still regarded as a success story in BPR terms, but the company is not yet out of the woods.

The problem remains that if rapid changes are introduced you have to be very fortunate if all aspects of the strategy work as intended. The pace of change affects the likely success of a project. It is important that a momentum is achieved but if the pace becomes excessive for the infrastructure the exercise will fail. What if the part of the organisation that was changed in BPR is essential to some other key process? There is a risk that in changing one process in a radical way it has a consequential and unforeseen impact on some other process. People could be left unable to handle changes because they had not been properly involved and the required training had not taken place (Oram and Wellins 1995).

In January 1996 (Davenport 1996) this point was dealt with by Tom Davenport who had been at the forefront of arguing the case for business process re-engineering. He declared that re-engineering was failing because it was 'a fad that forgot people'. This is a point made very strongly in the *People Management* article, which argues the case for looking at change with a consideration of its human aspects at the forefront. Perhaps the association of BPR with technology and processes has created its own worst problems. It is difficult to be so immersed in technology and processes while giving due weight to the people considerations. It is not realistic to flatten organisation structures and simply expect the people who remain to cope. What is the risk that unreasonable burdens will result? Can people be as flexible and infinitely malleable as BPR seems to suppose? Some, no doubt, can handle the change, but what of the casualties? Of course, BPR's supporters are aware of that and they stress that people, training, and other preparations for change must be fully thought through. The problem is that the consequences of major change makes such ideal considerations difficult to fulfil. The commitment to people that is at the heart of organisational philosophies on vision, culture and teamwork are difficult to square with large numbers of forced redundancies.

For BPR perhaps the problem has been the 'hype' that comes along with its forthright claims, and the desire to sweep away the past in radical change programmes. BPR has at its roots some excellent ideas shown in Table 56. The redesign of work processes and the use of technology is something that is gathering pace, hence showing its acceptability. The idea that work should be integrated and co-ordinated is a universal aim. The importance of capturing information only once is something that is well accepted, though not usually met in practice. The analysis of activities horizontally and where the process crosses a functional boundary are likewise important and recognised. Multi-skilling, empowerment, NIH, and the potential strains caused by functional power, are recognised along with a need to change in bite sized chunks. The problem is that while they are fundamental to BPR, they were not formulated there. Many of these ideas were fashioned in the 1950s in the Tavistock School and within the quality theories of W. Edwards Deming. What BPR has provided is the marketing push to thrust these ideas forward and provide them with focus. At the same time it has been seen as too reliant on a technical approach that treated human and organisational issues as 'little local difficulties'.

Table 56

THE IDEAS BEHIND BPR

☐	The redesign of work processes.
☐	The use of new technology.
☐	Integration and co-ordination of work.
☐	Information to be captured only once.
☐	Processes to be examined horizontally.
☐	Review where processes cross functions.
☐	Decisions to be taken at the lowest point in the organisation.
☐	Work to be multiskilled.
☐	Work to be regarded as an activity, not a task.
☐	Functional power can be dysfunctional.
☐	You can learn from others – be rid of NIH!
☐	Organisations are too complex to be changed in single steps.

The failures of BPR to accommodate the human and political dimensions in much of its practical application now means that the opportunity rests with us in HR. There is clearly a very big role waiting to be grasped here. Can the HR function provide that extra dimension that mingles efficiency with a respect for people? This is why this book has argued strongly for a strategic role for HR in reviewing not just the HR department but human aspects and endeavours across the whole organisation (Oram and Wellins 1995).

Summary and conclusion

At the same time as we read of the death of BPR, successes continue to emerge. A major British oil company is reported in the London *Financial Times* in December 1996 as having successfully completed a re-engineering exercise in one of its major oil platforms in the North Sea. This platform is a £2.5 billion business, itself big enough to make the FTSE 100. Perhaps there are those who have been too quick to write the obituary of BPR. Richard Lumb of Andersen Consulting believes that re-engineering is a response to unprecedented change. New technology and competitive pressures are rewriting the rule books of how organisations should be run and how changes should be handled.

The HR department can deliver a credible role in such strategic areas. We have to press upon managers that the long-term health of an organisation is at stake unless the people issues are thought through, and change is progressed in an integrated manner. Short-term cost-based solutions will create long-term problems, particularly in terms of the cynicism they create among people. Benchmarking requires that, and at times will look at the same issues as BPR. BPR is not dead if its narrow technical interpretation is avoided and the human aspects of change are fully taken into account. This is the challenge for HR people.

15

BENCHMARKING AND THE FUTURE

Benchmarking and business

Benchmarking has hit the business world in a big way. The idea that you should compare one organisation with another is not something that comes naturally to most people. Such are the differences in aims and objectives, and such are the complexities involved that unwilling people have 1001 excuses for not doing anything! Benchmarking is correctly seen as quite different from a simple comparison of statistics. Measurement is linear and logical, but assessing worth and deciding value is altogether a different proposition. We all recognise the power of the customer. Many companies come to benchmarking through intense competitive pressure. They see profits dwindling, budget cut upon budget cut, erosion of market share and failure of new products, while wistfully looking at competitors who seem to be doing things better. Matters are no easier for service organisations that receive the vast part of their cash from government rather than directly from customers. If customers do not perceive that they are getting a good service they can move to alternative suppliers. In these circumstances the money will move away with the client.

Where there is no financial exchange to determine success, attempts are being made to introduce artificial markets to have a similar, if lesser, effect. This is particularly the case in the health and education services, but it also applies to policing and social services. Resources are limited and demand is infinite, so whether you are in an oil company, retailing or manufacture, a police force or hospital or education, you are being benchmarked. If you let yourself slip and do not keep abreast of the changes, trouble is in store.

Comparing with others

Benchmarking has provided an opportunity for meeting the challenges of a fast changing environment. By comparing HR data with those of other organisations it is possible to take stock of your performance and practices and decide if any areas need particular attention. It is important, however, to recognise that in the HR area, particularly, comparisons based on metrics alone will have only limited value. However, it is reasonable to expect the metrics or numbers to serve as symptoms of what is happening within the organisation.

This limitation of a purely metric approach to benchmarking is particularly keen in the HR area. If you wish to make significant changes, sooner or later you have to compare processes. Does your reward strategy succeed better than another? What benefits in costs and service are gained by that organisation's way of working? How does that organisation organise itself to be so much more productive? These are the more difficult questions of process that HR must address.

Benchmarking is gradually becoming accepted across the whole field of business, government, services, schools, regulated utilities, local government and the rest. It gives information that allows organisations to assess priorities for change.

The experience of the education service with benchmarking is fascinating, and illustrative of the general tendency. Early tables of benchmarks were published in the 1980s in the teeth of vigorous opposition from much of the education service. Opposition was comprehensive, partly because the systems were new and imperfect, and partly because support had not been obtained first. This was made worse when errors were made in collecting the statistics.

In 1997 the situation is different. There are still articles that correctly show how tables can be manipulated (by getting all your students to sit A-level general studies or by seeking out the more generous examination boards, and so on!) but the tables are here to stay. The reality is that inside the education service people visit colleague schools and discover how they achieve better results. Is it resource allocation, teaching methods and so on? A revolution is quietly taking place. Away from the public glare people are learning from others. The measuring systems are improving gradually and confidence is growing in benchmarking. It is the same across the whole field of industry, commerce and government services.

Understanding context

One difficulty with ill-thought-out attempts at benchmarking is that the context is often ignored. It is absolutely necessary to understand context. You must have a clear understanding of where you are and what your history is. You cannot ignore these things. Sometimes it may be an advantage to what you are trying to do, but sometimes it will not. Managers know that some departments do better than others because they have advantages. That is not the point. The point is why some organisations within a similar environment and with a similar background seem to do so much better than others and whether you are showing any inclination to find out what managers expect of you, and to meet any shortcomings. This may require a willingness to think the unthinkable, such as whether to outsource or pass routine services to line managers or tackle trade unions or HR managers about complex procedures that serve to keep you in a job, but which do not meet customers' needs. It is far better to take the initiative in such areas rather than wait until line managers seek to throw out the baby with the bath-water and emasculate the whole HR activity. So HR departments must start benchmarking or improve the benchmarking they are already doing. Of course, there are reasons why something is not comparable and why the data look odd, but that is true of everything that is measured and counted – the metrics must not be applied unthinkingly.

One by one, benchmarking encourages reasons to be given and excuses to be made. Eventually comes the realisation that while such reasons are all true there is an overwhelming case that cannot be ignored. In the final analysis that organisation, or that school or hospital or that HR department is doing things better than you are.

The case for benchmarking

Benchmarking has received a boost from the easy availability of IT. As more expert systems become available more sophisticated ways of giving meaningful analysis naturally follow. But while IT fills a need, the ability to undertake analysis is not the driving force behind benchmarking. The push is being given by a world that is changing in all aspects of work at a pace that even 25 years ago would have seemed improbable. Within 14 years we have witnessed three or four major market developments in the use of home computers. Some changes are technically possible (for example, DAT technology for digital tape recording) but have been sidelined because the manufacturers fear domestic customers' rejection of another change, although its supporters say it is hugely superior to compact disc.

We have to invent practices that allow organisations to keep pace with this change. This is the point of benchmarking; it allows organisations to change artificially by engineering a development that is drawn from outside. This is the crucial contribution of benchmarking.

Benchmarking is here to stay. With the use of IT it becomes possible to include more and more information on more and more organisations. At the cursory level of basic statistics and league tables, they are now freely available across all areas of endeavour. They are published and available – the question is what your response will be.

Culture and people

Of course, the very artificiality of the change process brings inevitable strains with it. Change that does not evolve naturally from within the organisation must be introduced carefully and sensitively. This is the challenge for people managers – can they cultivate a culture where change is accepted as a natural part of business and where people are not continually threatened? The rhetoric has been all about people working 'smarter not harder', but if you speak to people on the ground it is the 'harder' rather than the 'smarter' that they are feeling most as processes are 're-engineered' – with the seemingly inevitable result of there being fewer people while more is asked of them.

Whither BPR?

This leads on to BPR. BPR has come in for a degree of criticism for all the reasons mentioned in Chapter 14. This author feels the criticism is overdone. What must happen is not the killing off of BPR but the humanising of it. This is a role for which HR departments are particularly suited. Understanding the effect on people of changes in processes, and the effect of changing employment levels on various activities, is something that the HR department is uniquely suited to carry out. Employees are not infinitely malleable commodities, who are indifferent to how they are managed or dealt with. That is why this book has laid such emphasis on mapping the organisation, on culture and on building support and understanding the difficulties that face employees.

Strategic frameworks

This must be carried out within a strategic framework. Benchmarking will not be effective if one-shot solutions to a variety of problems are attempted. The implications of change in one area on the efficiency of another must be thought through. The cultural as well as financial implications of change must also be considered. Too many organisations have implemented a lop-sided policy, where financial matters alone have determined policy. Typically, redundancies are implemented only to find after a period that the situation is as bad as it was before and more cuts become necessary. One reason this happens is because the decisions are taken based on only one part of the information. It is often not recognised that the very act of redundancy can break the spirit and morale of employees who no longer trust the organisation. Perhaps a fuller consideration of the human aspects will change the decisions, or change the manner and time-scale in which they are implemented.

Good-practice clubs

One problem that some users have found is that many companies are becoming overloaded with requests for comparative data and advice. This was why Xerox set up its own consulting arm to deal with the surge of requests that being a leading organisation inevitably attracts. This type of overloading of requests will gradually become more of an issue in the HR field. To deal with this we can expect clubs of the 'best practice' type to grow and flourish, whether run formally by consultants or established by groups of interested companies. Clubs are a convenient way to keep up to date in a fast-changing world. They provide an environment in which the latest ideas can be considered and investigated. Many of the problems that can be encountered (such as suspicion and the NIH problem) are likely to be avoided because they are supported by people who have an interest in benchmarking.

Benchmarking groups all have the same intention – to provide a ready forum to exchange information and ideas. They are an excellent approach and are to be encouraged. If you are not attached to one, search out the specialists in your area and they will put you in touch; they are the way forward. But there are other sources of help and support. Do not ignore your local IPD branch if you are a member. The IPD library services are also able to provide many of the benchmarking references listed in this book. Colleges, universities and technical libraries are an excellent and probably underused source of benchmarking information, particularly at the metric level.

HR starting at home

For HR to be able to stake their claim in the organisation requires those items which HR manages (which were discussed in Chapter 9) to be investigated. It is not appropriate to repeat them here, but one should be stressed. For HR to be taken seriously as a credible player in any corporate forum, it must first be running a tight and strategically focused department. For this reason the initiatives discussed in Chapter 9 are vitally important. HR must look critically at all the administrative and operational support functions that it carries out to see which should be outsourced or passed to line managers. Only when the HR department has a firm foundation based confidently on a clear, focused and coherent strategy can it hope or expect to be taken seriously. The issues that benchmarking throws up will be many and complex. Who will develop new methods in the future if we pass, say, recruitment and training to line managers? For example, if line managers controlled training who would have developed competences? Without the professional background and support that has been traditional, a new approach will be needed. Will HR departments be allowed by managers to set, and presumably audit, the standards that will guide day-to-day personnel operations? How competent will be the standard-setting by an HR strategy unit?

New ways to measure managerial performance

The new systems and processes will themselves create new problems, opportunities and challenges. We are already beginning to get a glimpse of the problems in terms of career development that flatter structures can create. Everywhere people ask where their promotion lines are in these new flatter structures. There is much to do for an HR unit that is focused on strategy. The problem is whether line managers will continue to review issues such as equal opportunities or employee relationships or development if the HR presence is lost on day-to-day operational personnel issues. Beyond such questions is the extent to which HR departments can be successful in ensuring that ethical considerations take their proper place in corporate decision-making.

What is required is a performance system that measures the healthy organisation, including employee morale and satisfaction and innovation. It appears that one may have been found in the 'balanced scorecard'. This measures and rewards a manager's performance based not just on traditional financial measures but also on approach to customers, with a third measure directed at learning, development and innovation and a fourth at employees and creating a healthy organisation. Such measures are a recognition that, with change being so rapid, other broader issues have to be measured. In the past such aspects may have taken care of themselves but this is no longer the case, if indeed it ever was. The jury is still out on whether such approaches will be successful. Will it be possible to come up with meaningful measures that give credibility to measurement beyond the narrow confines of traditional financial and short-term issues, such as last year's sales? The HR function has to be able to show that just as important to the long-term health and continuity of the company, are considerations of what is done now in training, recruitment and how people are treated.

This is the context in which benchmarking is being carried out. The search is on for good practice that is measurable and that can be implemented with the support of a willing workforce. A general called Sun-tzu in fourth-century BC China faced similar issues in his reputed work, *The Art of War.* He argued that societal considerations were as important as strictly military ones in fighting battles. He wrote:

> If you know your enemy and know yourself, you need not fear the result of a hundred battles.

In the business context the same principles hold true. You must know what you are good at, what you are bad at, what is going on and be able to measure so you can set improvement targets. This is what benchmarking can help you to achieve.

Appendix 1

METRICS FOR HR BENCHMARKING

This list of benchmark numerics has been provided by Saratoga (Europe) and is reproduced with their permission. It is a Benchmark Formulae Summary extract from their 1996 UK Human Resource Effectiveness report, which is available to subscribers. It is not suggested that you try to collect data for all of these measures at the early stage, but it will be helpful to look at the ratios and cost indicators to see what might be appropriate to your own circumstances. To become involved, contact Saratoga, whose address is given in Appendix 2. The second section suggests desirable positions to aim for.

A Organisational effectiveness

		Unit
1	Average revenue per FTE*	£ = Revenue divided by total FTE
2	Average costs per FTE	£ = Total costs divided by total FTEs
3	Average profit per FTE	£ = Pre-tax profit divided by total FTEs
4	Human investment ratio	£ = (Revenue – (Total costs – Total compensation & benefits) divided by (Total compensation & benefits)
5	Profit–Total Compensation	X :1 = Pre-tax profit divided by Total compensation
6	Profit–Variable Compensation	X :1 = Pre-tax profit divided by Variable compensation
7	Corporate overhead costs/Total costs	% = Corporate overhead costs divided by Total operating costs
8	Outsource agency costs/Total costs	% = Outsource agency costs divided by Total operating costs
9	Mgmt & prof. FTEs/Total FTEs	% = Mgmt & Prof. FTEs (Org) divided by Total FTEs

B HR staffing, costs and remuneration

1 FTEs per HR Dept FTE	X:1=	Total FTEs divided by Dept + Line HR FTEs
2 HR Dept costs per FTE	£ =	HR Dept costs divided by Total FTEs
3 FTEs per line HR FTEs	X:1=	Total FTEs divided by line HR FTEs
4 Line HR costs per FTE	£ =	Line HR costs divided by Total FTEs
5 FTEs per total HR FTEs	X:1=	Total FTEs divided by HR FTEs
6 Total HR costs per FTE	£ =	Total HR costs divided by Total FTEs
7 HR Outsource costs/HR Dept costs	% =	HR Outsource costs divided by HR Dept costs
8 Profit : Total HR costs	X : 1=	Profit divided by Total HR costs
9 HR Dept costs/Total costs	% =	HR Dept costs divided by Total costs
10 Mgmt & Prof. HR FTEs/All HR Dept FTEs	% =	Mgmt & Prof. Dept HR FTEs divided by Total HR Dept FTEs
11 Average HR Dept Compensation	£ =	Total HR Dept Compensation divided by Total HR Dept FTEs
12 FTEs per HR Dept FTE	X:1 =	Total FTEs divided by Dept + Line HR FTEs
13 HR Dept costs per FTE	£ =	Total HR Dept costs divided by Total FTEs
14 FTEs per line HR FTE	X:1=	Total FTEs divided by Total line HR FTEs
15 Line HR costs per FTE	£ =	Total Line HR costs divided by Total FTEs
16 FTEs per Total HR FTE	X:1=	Total FTEs divided by Total HR FTEs
17 Total HR Costs per FTE	£ =	Total HR Dept costs divided by FTEs
18 HR Outsource costs/HR Dept costs	% =	HR Outsource costs divided by HR Dept Costs
19 Profit : Total HR costs	X:1=	Pre-tax Profit divided by Total HR costs
20 HR Dept costs/Total costs	% =	HR Dept costs divided by Total costs
21 Mgmt & Prof HR FTEs/All HR Dept FTEs	% =	Mgmt & Prof HR FTEs divided by Total HR FTEs
22 Average HR Dept compensation	£ =	Total HR Dept compensation divided by Total HR FTEs

C Compensation and benefits

1a Compensation & Benefits/Revenue	% =	Total Compensation & Benefits divided by Total revenue
1b Compensation/Revenue	% =	Total Compensation divided by Total revenue
1c Benefits/Revenue	% =	Total Benefit Costs divided by Total revenue

2a Compensation & Benefits/Total costs	%	=	Total Benefits & costs divided by Total costs
2b Compensation/Total costs	%	=	Total Compensation divided by Total costs
2c Benefits/Total costs	%	=	Total Benefit Costs divided by Total costs
3a Average Remuneration (Comp & Ben)	£	=	Total Remuneration (Comp & Ben) divided by Total FTEs
3b Average Remuneration (Compensation)	£	=	Total Compensation divided by Total FTEs
3c Average Remuneration (Benefits)	£	=	Total benefit cost divided by Total FTEs
4 Total benefits/Total compensation	%	=	Total benefit cost divided by Total compensation

D Absence and turnover

1 Total absence rate	%	=	No. of Days All Absence divided by No. of FTE Workdays
2 Absence cost per FTE	£	=	(Total Absence Rate x Compensation) divided by FTEs
3 Non-scheduled absence rate	%	=	Casual days absence divided by No. of FTE Workdays
4 Non-scheduled absence cost per FTE	£	=	(Casual absence rate x Compensation) divided by FTEs
5 Termination rate	%	=	No. of terminations divided by headcount
6 Involuntary termination rate	%	=	No. of involuntary terminations divided by headcount
7 Voluntary termination rate	%	=	No. of voluntary terminations divided by headcount

8 Voluntary Termination Rate by Length of Service

i) 0-1 years in job)
ii) 1-3 years in job)
iii) 3-5 years in job) } % = { Total the No. of voluntary
iv) 5-10 years in job   terminations for each length
v) 10+ years in job   of service category and
                          divide by total No.
                          of voluntary terms

E Recruitment

1 External recruitment rate	%	=	No. of external recruits divided by headcount
2 External add rate	%	=	No. of external add recruits divided by headcount
3 External replacement rate	%	=	No. of external replacement recruits divided by headcount
4 Average cost per hire	£	=	(External recruiting cost + 10%) divided by No. recruited
5 Time to accept (external)	Days	=	No. of days to accept (external) divided by No. accepted
6 Acceptance rate (All)	%	=	No. of offers accepted divided by No. of Offers Made

F Training and development

1 Average training cost per FTE	£ =	Average training cost divided by total FTEs
1a In-house training cost per FTE	£ =	In-house training costs divided by total FTEs
1b External training cost per FTE	£ =	External training costs divided by Total FTEs
1c Training costs/Total compensation	% =	Total Training Costs divided by compensation cost
1d Training cost per hour	£ =	Total training cost divided by total hours
2 Average training cost per FTE	£ =	Total No. of training hours divided by total FTEs
2a In-house training cost per FTE	£ =	In-house training cost divided by total FTEs
2b External training cost per FTE	£ =	External cost divided by total FTEs
2c Training costs/total compensation	% =	Total training cost divided by compensation cost
2d Training cost per hour	£ =	Total training cost divided by total hours
3 Average training hours per FTE	Hours =	Total No. of training hours divided by total FTEs
3a In-house training hours per FTE	Hours =	No. of In-house training hours divided by total FTEs
3b External training hours per FTE	Hours =	No. of external training hours divided by total FTEs
3c Operational training hours per FTE	Hours =	No. of operational training hours divided by total FTEs
3d Developmental training hours per FTE	Hours =	No. of developmental training hours divided by total FTEs

G Occupational health and safety

1 Total OH&S costs per FTE	£ =	Total OH&S costs divided by total FTEs
2 Preventive OH&S costs per FTE	£ =	Preventive OH&S costs divided by total FTEs
3 Liability & rehab OH&S costs/ per FTE	£ =	Employer's liability & rehabilitation OH&S costs divided by total FTEs
4 Average lost time rate/incident	Days =	Current period days lost divided by current period occurrences
5 Lost time occurrences per 1,000 FTEs	% =	lost time occurrences divided by FTEs multiplied by 1,000
Measure:		**Desirable organisation position**** (all things to be equal)

A Organisational effectiveness

1	Average revenue per FTE	TOP 25
2	Average cost per FTE	BOTTOM 25
3	Average profit per FTE	TOP 25
4	Human investment ratio	TOP 25
5	Profit: total compensation	TOP 25
6	Profit: variable compensation	Organisation-specific
7	Corporate overhead costs/total costs	Organisation-specific
8	Outsource agency costs/Total costs	Organisation-specific
9	Mgmt & prof FTEs/Total FTEs	Organisation-specific

B HR staffing costs and remuneration

1	FTEs per HR Dept FTEs	TOP 25 – 40
2	HR Dept costs per FTE	BOTTOM 25 – 40
3	FTEs per line HR FTEs	TOP 25 – 40
4	Line HR costs per FTE	BOTTOM 25 – 40
5	FTEs per total HR FTEs	TOP 25 – 40
6	Total HR costs/FTE	BOTTOM 25 – 40
7	HR outsource costs/HR Dept cost	Organisation-specific
8	Profit: total HR costs	TOP 25
9	HR Dept costs/Total costs	BOTTOM 25 – 40
10	Mgmt & Prof HR FTEs/All HR Dept FTEs	TOP 25
11	Average HR Dept compensation	TOP 10 – 40
12	FTEs per HR Dept FTE	TOP 25 – 40
13	HR Dept costs per FTE	BOTTOM 25 – 40
14	FTEs per line HR FTE	TOP 25 – 40
15	Line HR costs per FTE	BOTTOM 25 – 40
16	FTEs per total HR FTE	TOP 25 – 40
17	Total HR costs per FTE	BOTTOM 25 – 40
18	HR outsource cost/HR Dept cost	Organisation-specific
19	Profit: Total HR costs	TOP 25
20	HR Dept costs/total costs	BOTTOM 25 – 40
21	Mgmt & prof HR FTEs/All HR Dept FTEs	TOP 25
22	Average HR Dept compensation	Organisation-specific

C Compensation and Benefits

1a	Compensation & benefits/Revenue	BOTTOM 25
1b	Compensation/Revenue	BOTTOM 25
1c	Benefits/Revenue	Organisation-specific
2a	Compensation & benefits/Total costs	BOTTOM 25
2b	Compensation/Total costs	BOTTOM 25
2c	Benefits/Total costs	Organisation-specific
3a	Average remuneration (Comp & Ben)	TOP 10 – 40

3b Average remuneration (Compensation)   TOP 10 – 40
3c Average remuneration (Benefits)   Organisation-specific
4   Total benefits/Total compensation   Organisation-specific

D Absence and turnover

1 Total absence rate	BOTTOM 25
2 Absence cost per FTE	BOTTOM 25
3 Non-scheduled absence rate	BOTTOM 25
4 Non-scheduled absence cost per FTE	BOTTOM 25
5 Termination tate	BOTTOM 25
6 Involuntary termination rate	Organisation-specific
7 Voluntary termination rate	BOTTOM 25
8 Voluntary termination rate by length of service	
i) 0-1 years in job	BOTTOM 25
ii) 1-3 years in job	BOTTOM 25
iii) 3-5 years in job	Organisation-specific
iv) 5-10 years in job	Organisation-specific
v) 10+ years in job	Organisation-specific

E Recruitment

1 External recruitment rate	Organisation-specific
2 External add rate	Organisation-specific
3 External replacement rate	Organisation-specific
4 Average cost per hire	BOTTOM 30 – 50
5 Time to accept (external)	BOTTOM 25
6 Acceptance rate (All)	TOP 25
7 Temporary recruiting cost per hire	BOTTOM 30 – 50

F Training development

1 Average training cost per FTE	TOP 20 – 40
1a In-house training cost per FTE	TOP 20 – 40
1b External training cost per FTE	TOP 20 – 40
1c Training costs/total compensation	TOP 20 – 40
1d Training cost per hour	TOP 20 – 40
2 Average training cost per FTE	TOP 20 – 40
2a In-house training cost per FTE	TOP 20 – 40
2b External training cost per FTE	TOP 20 – 40
2c Training costs/Total compensation	TOP 20 – 40
2d Training cost per hour	Organisation-specific
3 Average training hours per FTE	TOP 20 – 40
3a In-house training hours per FTE	TOP 20 – 40
3b External training hours per FTE	TOP 20 – 40
3c Operational training hours per FTE	TOP 20 – 40
3d Development training hours per FTE	TOP 20 – 40

G Occupational health and safety

1 Total OH&S costs per FTE	Organisation-specific
2 Preventive OH&S Costs per FTE	Organisation-specific
3 Liability & rehab OH&S costs per FTE	BOTTOM 25
4 Average lost time rate/Incident	BOTTOM 25
5 Lost Time Occurrences per 1,000 FTEs	BOTTOM 25

* FTE = 'full time equivalent employee'.

** Desirable **organisation** position assumes 'all things being equal' in terms of cost, time, quality, quantity and human reaction.

APPENDIX 2

LIST OF BENCHMARKING CONTACTS

The following organisations are either those with which I have had personal business experience or who gave assistance freely during preparation of this book, in most cases both. They are well worth contacting to ascertain the services that they can offer your organisation. This is not to ignore the large number of other consultancies that exist and which provide services in this area, such as KPMG, McKinsey, and Xerox Quality Solutions, with which I have not happened to come in contact.

1   Institute of Personnel and Development
      Library and Information Services
      Camp Road
      London SW19 4UX
      The IPD library holds many of the references listed in this book. Others are available from other abstracts service providers or from the author.

2   Saratoga (Europe)
      65 Church Street
      Lancaster LA1 1ET

3   Coopers & Lybrand
      Plumtree Court
      London EC4A 4HT

4   British Quality Foundation
      215 Vauxhall Bridge Road
      London SW1V 1EN

5   Pilat UK
      29 Hendon Lane
      London N1 3PZ

6   Ward Dutton Partnership
    20 Chishill Road
    Heydon, Royston
    Hertfordshire SG8 8PW
7   Electoral Reform Ballot Services
    Market Research Department
    33 Clarendon Road
    London N8 ONW
8   Senn Delaney Leadership Consulting Group
    3780 Kilroy Airport Way
    Long Beach
    California 90806
    Tel:USA 310-426-5400
9   Incomes Data Services
    Pay Benchmarking Database
    193 St John's Street
    London EC1V 4LS
10 TQM International
    The Stables, Tarvin Road
    Frodsham
    Cheshire WA6 6XN
11 Best Practice Club
    Wolseley Business Park
    Kempston
    Bedford MK42 7PW
12 Arthur Andersen
    Global Best Practices (PC Windows Introductory
    Software)
    c/o 2 Arundel Street
    London WC2R 3LT
13 Ernst & Young
    (Benchmarking by HJ Harrington PC Windows-based
    Software approach)
    Human Management Resourcing
    Rolls House
    7 Rolls Building
    Fetter Lane
    London
    EC4A 1NH

REFERENCES
AND FURTHER READING

ADAMS S. (1994) 'How well do we do?' *Occupational Health*. Vol.46, No.11. November. pp373–5.

AMERICAN PRODUCTIVITY AND QUALITY CENTRE. (1993) *The Benchmarking Management Guide*. Productivity Press, 1993.

ANDERSON B. *and* CAMP R.C. (1995) 'Current position and future development of benchmarking'. *TQM Magazine*. Vol.7, No.5.

ARMSTRONG M. (1996) *Employee Reward*. London, IPD.

BEE R. *and* F. (1997) *Project Management: The people challenge*. London, IPD.

'Benchmarking and managing labour turnover'. (1996) *IRS Employment Review: Employee Development Bulletin*. No.604. March.

'Benchmarking for success; identifying competitive practices'. (1993) *Industrial Relations Review and Report*. No.537. June. pp5–7.

'Benchmarking management development processes'. (1994) *Industrial Relations Review and Report; Employee Development Bulletin*. No.562. June. pp10–12.

BENDELL T., BOULTER L. *and* KELLY J. (1993) *Benchmarking for Competitive Advantage*. London, Pitman.

BENDELL T., KELLY J., *and* MERRY T. (1993) *Quality: Measuring and monitoring*. London, Century Business.

BOGAN C.E. *and* ENGLISH M.J. (1994) *Benchmarking for Best Practices*. New York, McGraw-Hill Inc.

BOWMAN C. *and* FAULKNER D. (1994) 'Measuring product advantage using competitive benchmarking and customer perceptions'. *Long Range Planner*. Vol.27, No.1. February.

BOXWELL, R.J. (1994) *Benchmarking for Competitive Advantage*. Maidenhead, McGraw-Hill.

BRACKEN D.W. (1992) 'Benchmarking employee attitudes'.

Training and Development (USA). Vol.46, No.6. June. pp49–53.

BRAMHAM J. (1988) *Practical Manpower Planning.* London, IPM.

BRAMHAM J. (1994) *Human Resource Planning.* 2nd edn. London, IPD.

BRAMHAM J. (1996) *Report of Michael Hammer's 1995 Benchmarking Conference to TransCo.* Knaresborough. (Out of print but available to students from the author.)

BRECKLEY C. (1996) 'Teamworking in Royal Mail'. *The Times.*

BROOKS R. *and* WRAGG T. (1996) 'Benchmark for the best business'. *Managing Service Quality.* September. pp13–16.

BROWN M. (1996) 'Benchmarking conundrums'. *Benchmarking Conundrums.* September–October. pp112–14.

BURN D.A. (1993) 'Benchmarking for quality in personnel'. *Quality in the Personnel Function.* 24 November.

BURNS T. and STALKER G.N. (1961) *The Management of Innovations.* London, Tavistock Publications.

CAMP R.C. (1989) *Benchmarking: The search for industry best practices that lead to superior performance.* Milwaukee, Wisconsin, American Society for Quality Control (ASQC).

CAMP R.C. (1993) 'A bible for benchmarking at Xerox'. *Financial Executive.* Vol.9, No.4. July–August. pp23–7.

CAMP R.C. (1995) *Business Process Benchmarking: Finding and implementing best practices.* Milwaukee, Wisconsin, American Society for Quality Control (ASQC).

CAPPELLI P. and CROCKER-HEFTER A. (1996) 'Distinctive human resources are firms' core competencies'. *Organisational Dynamics.* Vol.24, No.3. Winter. pp7–22.

CARRINGTON L. (1994) 'Measure for measure'. *Personnel Today.* 14–27 June. pp37-8.

CHAMPY J. (1995) *Re-Engineering Management.* London, HarperCollins.

CHANG R.Y. *and* KELLY P.K. (1995) *Improving through Benchmarking: A practical guide to achieving peak process performance.* London, Kogan Page.

CHILDRESS J.R. *and* SENN L.E. (1995) *In The Eye Of The Storm.* Los Angeles, Leadership Press.

CHINATA Y. (1994) 'Benchmarking: the Japanese experience'. *Long Range Planning.* Vol.27, No.4. August. pp48–53.

CLARK F.A. (1992) *Quality and Service: A key focus for performance in the public sector.* Henley, Henley Management College.

CODLING S. (1992) *Best Practice Benchmarking: The management guide.* Industrial Newsletters.

CONFEDERATION OF BRITISH INDUSTRY. (1995) *World Hosts: International benchmarking in the hospitality industry.* Confederation of British Industry.

CONFEDERATION OF BRITISH IINDUSTRY *and* COOPERS & LYBRAND. (1993) *Survey of Benchmarking in the UK: Executive summary, 1993.* Confederation of British Industry.

COOPERS & LYBRAND *and* CONFEDERATION OF BRITISH INDUSTRY. (1994) *Survey of Benchmarking in the UK: Executive summary 1994.* Coopers & Lybrand.

CREELAND J. (1996) 'A balanced perspective'. *Best Practice IFS International Ltd.* September. pp17–19.

CROSS M. (1995) *The Benchmarking Sourcebook.* Michael Cross.

DAVENPORT T. (1992) *Process Innovation: Re-engineering work through information technology.* Cambridge, Mass., Harvard Business School Press.

DAVENPORT T. (1996) 'Why re-engineering failed: the fad that forgot people'. *Harvard Business Review* January–February.

DAY L. *and* OVERMYER E. (1995) 'Benchmarking training'. *Training and Development (USA).* Vol.49, No.11. November. pp27-30.

DOLAN S. (1995) 'A different use of natural sources'. *People Management.* Vol.1, No. 20. 5 October. pp36–7, 39–40.

DOLPHIN R. (1996) 'Managing and benchmarking employee benefits'. *Topics.* No.67. pp15–18.

FISSING (Financial Services Special Interest Group of the Manpower Society). (1997) *Benchmarking for Better Human Resource Management.* Bournemouth, Report No. 30.

FITZ-ENZ J. (1984) *How To Measure Human Resource Management.* Maidenhead, McGraw-Hill.

FITZ-ENZ J. (1990) *Human Value Management.* San Francisco, Jossey Bass.

FITZ-ENZ J. (1993) *Benchmarking Staff Performance.* San Francisco, Jossey Bass.

FITZ-ENZ J. (1993) 'How to make benchmarking work for you'. *HR Magazine.* Vol.38, No.12. December. pp40–47.

FONDA N. and BUCKTON K. (1995) *Reviewing the Personnel Function: A toolkit for development.* London, Institute of Personnel and Development.

FORD D.J. (1993) 'Benchmarking HRD'. *Training and Development (USA).* Vol.47. No.6. June.

GAMMIE A. (1993) 'Performance measurement and the role of benchmarking'. *Topics.* No.57. Winter–spring.

GLANZ E.F. and DAILEY L.K. (1992) 'Benchmarking'. *Human Resource Management.* Vol.31, Nos.1–2. Spring–summer.

HALL L. (1995) 'Factory models'. *Personnel Today.* 7 November. pp35–6.

HAMMER M. and CHAMPY J. (1994) *Re-Engineering the Corporation.* London, Nicholas Brealey.

HILTROP J.M. and DESPRES C. (1994) 'Benchmarking the performance of human resource management'. *Long Range Planning.* Vol. 27, No. 6. pp43–57.

HOLLINGS L. (1992) 'Clearing up the confusion'. *TQM Magazine.* Vol.4, No.3. June. pp149–51.

HOLLOWAY J., LEWIS J. and MALLORY G. (1995) *Performance Measurement and Evaluation.* London, Sage; Milton Keynes, Open University.

HOLT B. (1994) 'Benchmarking comes to HR'. *Personnel Management,* Vol.26, No.8. June. pp32–5.

HOULDER V. (1994) 'Measuring up to success'. *The Financial Times.* 1 August. London.

INCOMES DATA SERVICES. (1992) 'Multi-skilling and teamworking extended at BP, Baglan Bay'. *Incomes Data Services Report.* No.631. December. pp29–32.

INCOMES DATA SERVICES. (1995) *Pay Benchmarking.* London, IDS.

INCOMES DATA SERVICES. (1997) *Measuring Personnel Effectiveness.* Study No. 618. London, IDS.

JOYCE M.E. (1995) *How to Lead Your Business beyond TQM.* London, Pitman.

KAPLAN R.S. and NORTON D.P. (1993) 'Measuring corporate performance – the balanced scorecard'. *Harvard Business School Management Production.*

KARLOF, B. and OSTBLOM S. (1993) *Benchmarking: A signpost*

to excellence in quality and productivity. Chichester, John Wiley.

KENT S. (1995) 'Policy of competition'. *Personnel Today.* 21 November. pp37, 39–40.

LABOUR RESEARCH DEPARTMENT (LRD) SURVEY. (1995) *Guide to New Management Techniques.* London, LRD.

LEEMAN R. (1996) 'An Abbey National Habit'. *Management Services.* Vol.40, No.3. March. pp14–17.

LOWE K. (1994) 'Test pilots'. *Personnel Today.* 9–29 August. pp25–7.

'Management Development: Benchmarking'. (1994) *Industrial Relations Review and Report.* No.562. June. London.

MARCHINGTON M. and WILKINSON A. (1996) *Core Personnel and Development.* London, IPD.

MAYO A. and LANK E. (1994) *The Power of Learning: A guide to gaining competitive advantage.* London, Institute of Personnel and Development.

MCNAIR C.J. and LEIBFRIED K.H.J. *Benchmarking: A tool for continuous improvement.* London, Harper Business.

MCNULTY T. (1993) 'Benchmarking how to launch a project and get results'. *Croner Employer's Briefing.* No.48. 16 November.

MCNULTY T. (1993) 'Benchmarking: what is it and is it right for you?'. *Croner Employer's Briefing.* No.47. 1 November p.6.

MUMFORD E. and HENDRICKS R. (1996) 'Business process re-engineering RIP'. *People Management.* 22–7 May.

O'REILLY N. (1995) 'Hard measures'. *Personnel Today.* 26 September. pp33–4.

ORAM M. and WELLINS R.S. (1995) *Re-engineering's Missing Ingredient: The human factor.* London, IPD.

OVERMAN S. (1993) 'In search of best practice'. *HR Magazine.* Vol.38, No.12. December. pp48–50.

PARKER N. and HARRISON P. (1995) *Benchmarking.* London, Institute of Management.

PENLEY K. (1991–92) 'Benchmarking: what it is and how to use it'. *Human Resources.* Issue 4. Winter.

PETERS T. and WATERMAN R. (1982) *In Search Of Excellence.* New York, Harper & Row. (For the antidote to Tom Peters, see also S. Crainer, *Corporate Man To Corporate Skunk: the Tom Peters phenomenon,* Capstone, 1997.)

PRICE WATERHOUSE. (1995) *Overview of the benchmarking process*. London, Price Waterhouse.

PROSPECT CENTRE. (1994) *An Introductory Guide to Benchmarking Human Resource Development*. Prospect Centre.

RENDELL T., BOULTER L. *and* KELLY J.(1993) *Benchmarking for Competitive Advantage*. London, Pitman.

RYLATT A. (1994) *Learning Unlimited: Practical strategies and techniques for transforming learning in the workplace*. Business and Professional.

SARATOGA (EUROPE (1996) 'Building competitive advantage through best practice benchmarking'. *Annual Benchmarking Conference*.

SCHOFIELD J. (1996) 'A secure outlook'. *Best Practice IFS International Ltd*. September. pp21–3.

SHETTY Y.K. (1993) 'Aiming high: competitive benchmarking for superior performance'. *Long Range Planning*. Vol.26, No.1. February. pp39–44.

SPENDOLINI M.J. (1992) *The Benchmarking Book*. New York, Amacom.

SPENDOLINI M.J. (1992) 'The benchmarking process'. *Compensation and Benefits Review*. Vol.24, No.5. September–October. pp21–9.

STEEL TRAINING LIMITED. (1995) *The Contribution of Training to Business Competitiveness: Report of a benchmarking project between 16 UK industry companies; Vol. 1 – The UK Experience*. Steel Training.

TOLOND C. (1995) 'Health check'. *Personnel Today*. 26 September. pp36–8.

TUTCHER G. (1994) 'How successful companies improve through internal benchmarking'. *Managing Service Quality*. Vol.4, No.2. pp44–6.

ULRICH D., BROCKBANK W. *and* YEUNG A. (1989) 'Beyond belief: a benchmark for human resources'. *Human Resource Management*. Vol.28, No.3. pp311–35.

ULRICH D. *et al.* (1989) 'Benchmarking for human resources'. *Human Resource Management*. Vol. 28, No. 3. pp331-5.

VAN DE VLIET A. (1995) 'Benchmarking HR management'. *Human Resources*. No.18 May–June. pp46–8, 50.

VAZIRI H.K. (1993) 'Questions to answer before benchmarking'. *Planning Review*. Vol. 21, No. 37. January–February.

WATSON G. H. (1993) *Strategic Benchmarking: How to rate your company's performance against the world's best*. Chichester, John Wiley.

WHEATLEY J.D. (1992) 'Dare to compare for better productivity'. *HR Magazine*. Vol.37, No 9. September. pp42–6.

WILLIAMS M. (1996) 'Verifying the service'. *Best Practice IFS International Ltd*. September. pp53–5.

WILLMOTT H. (1994) 'Business process re-engineering and human resource management'. *Personnel Review*. Vol.23, No.3.

WIMPRESS D. (1996) 'Opinion'. *Personnel Today*. 27 August.

ZAIRI M. (1992) *Competitive Benchmarking: An executive guide*. Technical Communications.

ZAIRI M. (1994) 'Demistifying the art of benchmarking'. *Training Officer*. Vol.30, No.6. July–August. pp187–90.

ZAIRI M. (1996) 'Competition: what does it mean?'. *TQM Magazine*. Vol.8, No.1. pp54–9.

ZAIRI M. and HUTTON R. (1995) 'Benchmarking: a process-driven tool for quality improvement'. *TQM Magazine*. Vol.7, No.3. pp35–40.

ZAIRI M. and LEONARD P. (1994) *Practical Benchmarking: The complete guide*. London, Chapman and Hall.

INDEX